GW00656009

RACING

EVERY WEEK WE RECEIVE 1st CLASS INFORMATION FROM SOME VERY SHREWD PEOPLE. HERE ARE A FEW OF OUR WINNERS LISTED BELOW

FIRM LANDING	WON	25-1
SHADES OF LIGHT	WON	20-1
TACTICCIO	WON	14-1
MULTUM IN PARVO	WON	12-1
MIAMI IN SPRING	WON	12-1
CHURCH WARDEN	WON	12-1
AMIGO·MENOR	WON	11-1
MINIZEN LASS	WON	10-1
TEAM EFFORT	WON	8-1
MASTER PLAN	WON	6-1
BLAZING WALKER	WON	4-1
IN THE GROOVE	WON	9-2
JUNK BOND	WON	4-1
ON HIS OWN	WON	4-1
SEAGRAM	WON	3-1
BOLANEY BOY	WON	5-2
KNOCKBRACK	WON	9-4
BELMOREDEAN	WON	15-8
AQUILIFER	WON	7-4

Plus many more winners

If you had backed all our horses including the small number of losers with a £100 stake you would have made over **£25,000 profit!**

OUR TERMS FOR OUR FIRST CLASS SATURDAY PHONE SERVICE ARE:
£20 for one, £35 for two, £45 for three, £75 for six
One horse but never more than two will be given usually on Saturdays

TURN THE TABLES ON YOUR BOOKMAKER NOW!

Please send Cheque/P.O. to:-
GOLDLINE RACING
243 Bury Old Road, Bury, Lancs., BL9 7JB
ENQUIRIES WELCOME, MOBILE – 0860 922 314

...m to do winner. I managed to take a price of 20·1 on the horse. I have enclosed a cheque for your next three advices.

I would also like to say that this is the first time I have ever received three winners on the trot especially at these prices.

Dear Goldline,

I must write to thank you, your last winner paid for a holiday in FIJI, the result today made me nearly £50,000 in front. I shall use the winnings to buy my 19 year old daughter her own flat. Many thanks to you.

Dear Sir,

I enclose a cheque for £45.00 for another 3 Saturdays on your service. Yours is the first service that I have subscribed to which has made a profit after receiving the advices. Usually the services lose, then start winning after my subscription lapses. Keep up the good work.

Dear Sir,

May I take this opportunity to thank you for the excellent win you gave me on the two horses you advised me to back on Saturday, your information was exceptionally accurate.

Dear Sir,

Many thanks for Blazing Walker. I had a good bet at 5·1, your information was superb, thanks again.

Dear Sir,

Thank you very much for the information you gave last Saturday. I was able to secure a good price in the morning Bolaney Boy.

STOP PRESS:

KATABATIC WON 4-1

OVERSEAS CLIENTS WELCOME

New edition

KNOW YOUR BETS

By David Bennett

A Sporting Life Guide

© 1992 David Bennett

Published by The Sporting Life
Orbit House, 1 New Fetter Lane, London EC4A 1AR

First edition 1989
Reprinted 1990
New edition, revised and updated, 1992

ISBN 0 901091 50 2

Text typeset by Cotswold Typesetting Ltd, Cheltenham
Cover origination by Reprosharp Ltd, London EC1
Cover printed by Ark Litho, London SW19
Text printed and bound by The Bath Press, Bath

Picture credits
Cover upper left, *The Sporting Life*; cover lower right, Paul
Duffett (*The Sporting Life*); p. 18, author's collection

Acknowledgements
The author expresses thanks to the following companies for
assistance kindly provided: (in alphabetical order) American
Sports Betting Service, City Index, Coral, Ladbrokes, Super
Soccer, the Tote, and William Hill. Also to the numerous
other organisations who kindly answered queries and provided information.

Introduction
Thinking clearly about betting

Everybody knows bookmakers make profits. The only way such profits can be made is through the losses of their customers. It is evident, therefore, that although bettors may claim to have 'winning' as an objective, few can truly claim to win (in a long-term sense) in practice.

Since it is not reasonable to suppose that the betting public, as a whole, is irrational, one can conclude that betting, by-and-large for most people, is a recreational activity, carried on for the excitement, entertainment, suspense, feeling of participation in the sporting event, or some other subjective gain. The difference between the money staked by the bettor and the money returned in winnings – that is to say, the cost of betting – is regarded by the bettor (albeit not necessarily consciously) as a payment for the enjoyment gained from the betting experience.

However, notwithstanding these subjective criteria, the objective criterion of hoped-for gain is both a nominal goal, even for recreational bettors, and an actual goal for a smaller though sizeable group of bettors who strive, in ways realistic or unrealistic, to turn betting into a gainful form of labour!

Essentially, there are two ways in which real gain can be pursued through the medium of horse racing or other sports betting.

The first is through bets with a high winnings-to-stakes ratio, that is to say accumulators or multiple bets at very long, possibly astronomical, odds. Sums of up to £$\frac{1}{2}$ million can be won in this way and a person lucky enough to scoop such a payout (provided he does not thereafter squander his winnings in an extravagant betting spree) is likely truly to be able to claim that his betting has paid off. Even a person whose betting consists of, say, just £1 wagered every weekend on a long-odds accumulator for 30 years has a betting balance-sheet in black rather than red if ever he succeeds in landing odds of, say, a mere 2,000/1!

Those who win such big payouts are, of course, a lucky few. Their winnings, and the dividends for book-makers' shareholders, are paid for by the unlucky majority whose lifelong pursuit of a big accumulative win adds up to a lifelong loss! Even so, such bettors have the enjoyment of the anticipation and excitement which the hope of a big payout provides.

The second way in which the goal of gain can be pursued is by trying to turn betting into a 'favourable game' (see p. 35). A favourable game exists where the payout-odds on offer for a given outcome under-estimate its likelihood of occurring. 'Heads' in a coin-spinning game is an evens (1/1) chance. If a bene-factor were willing to pay odds of 6/5 every time 'heads' was correctly called, a game favourable to the caller would exist. Naturally, in the real world of betting, such favourable odds or 'overlays' are not going to be so transparently obvious!

Given that the betting industry has its own profits – not those of its customers – to consider, it is only to be expected that bookmakers should strive to avoid inadvertently offering such overlays. However, by virtue of its nature, volume and sheer complexity, bookmaker betting is bound to throw up, from time to time, odds favourable to the bettor. Any person in a position to recognise such value (see p. 122) and who limits his bets solely to those occasions is able, in effect, to turn betting with a bookmaker into a favourable game.

However, the bettor can only find favourable betting opportunities if he possesses sufficient ability to weigh the chances of the contenders and make reliable comparisons with the odds on offer. There are many reasons why payout-odds, on occasions, do not correspond with a contender's chance, but to be able to recognise such differences requires a mind educated in the sport in question and in the abilities of its players.

The bettor's own brain is his great ally in this process. It is a natural opinion-forming machine which tends to perform qualitatively in proportion to the amount and soundness of relevant information made available to it. It does not, of course, generate its opinions in numbers which can be directly compared with prices but, with practice, it is rapidly capable of learning to calibrate different strengths of belief against odds on offer. It is absurd that bettors should expect that collections of simple rules called 'systems' should be capable of outperforming the in-built reasoning and integrative powers of the human mind.

However, the reasoning machinery of the brain does have an opponent – emotional bias (which stems from a separate biological system) – which, in betting matters, must necessarily be resisted. When a team, jockey, player or whatever gives the would-be bettor a 'warm feeling', emotion is at work. Bettors should be on their guard and forbear from betting on the basis of any such impulse. It has to be said, some people so habitually run on their emotions in everything they do, this is a lesson they are for ever unable to learn. That actually works in favour of the value-seeking bettor: whenever a tide of emotional feeling for a given contender engulfs the betting market, favourable odds are created for a more able contender who does not so arouse public passion!

In addition to being able to form sound judgements, free of bias, about the chances of contenders, the bettor needs a basic understanding of certain arithmetical and mathematical issues. For example, be able to recognise or work out bookmakers' overall profit margins, since the bettor is more likely to experience a productive betting campaign if, at the outset, he concentrates on events where the 'over-round' is low. This is a topic fully explained under appropriate headings elsewhere in this book (see, for example, p. 69).

Similarly, there are certain mathematical axioms that must necessarily be heeded. Some may be difficult for a non-mathematically inclined person to understand. This need not in itself matter, so long as the principle is accepted and followed. Certain such principles are counter-intuitive, such as those relating to staking policy.

Mathematical axioms for unfavourable games may be different for favourable games, often going into reverse. For example, if a bettor makes an accumulative bet out of odds each of which is individually unfavourable, the margin in favour of the bookmaker multiplies, so that the bettor so wagering loses his funds at a faster rate. However, if a bettor's accumulative bet is made up of favourable odds (*ie* overlays), the margin in the bettor's favour multiplies to his own advantage and he thereby wins at a faster rate. The difficulty of finding several favourable betting opportunities at one time is clearly a limiting factor.

Bettors should not overestimate the possibilities for gainful betting. Good play, in itself, does not guarantee gain because the bookmakers' in-built margin (and, off-course, 'tax') often set up a spread which cannot be covered. The term 'better-than-average' is frequently used in this book to describe a betting performance, not necessarily a gainful one, whereby less is paid to bookmakers' profits than is prescribed by the in-built overall margin.

Better-than-average performance is a worthwhile objective for all bettors, even those who are purely recreational, since the cost of betting is thereby lessened and the betting pound buys more entertainment. For those who are not satisfied by the recreational uses of betting alone, better-than-average is a step closer to the ideal of an actual gain.

While a bettor's expectations, in terms of gain, should not be too great, a long-term profit of a few percentage points is mathematically attainable, even off-course, but it involves harnessing the troika of judgement, personal psychology and mathematical wisdom. The purpose of this book is to bring together relevant information in all these fields, as well as facts about betting shop rules and the bets available, to enable bettors to pursue their betting objectives effectively, whatever those objectives may be.

For readers committed to achieving 'better-than-average' results, the following is a summary of principles based on the theory of betting as presented in this book:

(1) Hone expertise by specialising in one or two chosen sports only.

(2) Be selective. Do not expect a betting opportunity from every contest. It is to be expected that there

should be more non-betting than betting occasions.

(3) Learn the finer points of a sport from observation. Choose a sport that can be watched 'live' or 'live' on television.

(4) Be properly informed with up-to-date news and information before making a wager. In the case of sports betting, read the specialised press.

(5) Assimilate expert opinion, but always from more than one viewpoint, preferably several.

(6) Rid the mind of emotional bias.

(7) Bet only if the odds appear favourable.

(8) Bet as close as reasonably possible to the start of the contest, in order to assimilate the latest information.

(9) Bet the smallest affordable stake that is sufficient to motivate and sustain interest, and bet as often as good opportunities allow. It is a dangerous fallacy to believe that a better return can be obtained from betting by increasing the sums staked. Increasing the amount risked introduces stress to the betting situation which, in turn, impairs the bettor's judgement, while at the same time increasing the mathematical likelihood of 'ruin' (see p. 95). The bettor who wants to make a real gain from betting must settle for a modest one!

There are many whose knowledge of racing or other sport would naturally qualify them to make gain from betting who nevertheless fail – because they regard mathematical tenets as irrelevant, or are unable to resist the psychological pressure to bet when they know they should not, or, out of a desire to win big money, fatally put at risk too much in stakes.

Useful tables in text

Notes

(1) Many of the entries in this book explain the workings of book-makers' rules. But because rules may vary from firm to firm, the version given in the book does not necessarily hold true in every case but represents what is believed to be a usual form.

(2) A bettor, bookmaker or other person associated with betting may, of course, be a man or woman. The use of the pronoun 'he' throughout the text should therefore be understood to mean 'he' or 'she'.

Abbreviations

A-T-C   Any-to-come
BAGS   Bookmakers' Afternoon Greyhound Services Ltd
BOLA   Betting Office Licensees Association
CSF   Computer straight forecast
D/F   Dual-forecast
D-S-A   Double-stakes-about
ED   Equally-divided
EW   Each-way
FAV   Favourite
F/C   Forecast
FPP   First past the post
HTB   Horserace Totalisator Board
LBO   Licensed Betting Office
NAB   National Association of Bookmakers
NGRC   National Greyhound Racing Club
NSL   National Sporting League
RR   Racing rules (inadvisably 'Round Robin', which should be written in full)
R-T-C   Round-the-clock
SIS   Satellite Information Services Ltd
SP   Starting price
S-S-A   Single-stakes-about
T-T-C   Through-the-card
T   Trap (T5 = Trap 5)

Accumulator

An 'accumulative bet', or 'accumulator', is a wager consisting of two or more selections in which the return (winnings+stake) from each successive 'leg' is automatically re-staked on the next. If there is a losing leg, the wager fails. Accumulators are known as 'doubles', 'trebles', 'fourfolds', and so on, depending on the number of legs.

Linking bets together in accumulators necessarily makes it much more difficult to win. A treble consisting of 3 one-in-3 chances has an overall chance of only one-in-27 of succeeding. The bettor considering accumulators must therefore be prepared to experience many disappointing near-misses while waiting for a bonanza!

Since some accumulators, if successful, may land substantial odds, bettors should check beforehand that the bookmaker's payout limits are sufficient to assure that winnings will be paid in full. Accumulative odds may be calculated in the manner shown in the panel on p. 14.

Bettors should also be wary of 'across-the-card' limits – a special limitation on payouts, imposed by some, mainly smaller, firms on accumulative bets involving successful selections in events run within a certain interval (say, 15 minutes or less) of each other. Thus, a fivefold consisting of bets at 1.30, 1.45, 2.30, 3.00 and 3.30 could, where a 15-minute across-the-card restriction applied, be liable to the special limit on account of the bets at 1.30 and 1.45.

Likewise, accumulative bets including an event run outside betting shop hours may be subject to a similar, if not more restricting, payout limit. Check the rules!

From the bookmaker's point of view, especially if the firm is a small one, such rules are necessary as a protection against excessive liabilities incurred under circumstances which make the normal mechanism of 'laying-off' liability difficult or impossible.

Accumulators may be 'win only' or 'each-way'. Normally, each-way accumulators are settled win-to-win and place-to-place. But in some regions, 'equally-divided settlement' is customary. By this method, the total return, win and place, of each leg is equally-divided and re-staked, half for a win and half for a place, on the next leg. The methods obviously produce different returns. Which is more favourable depends upon the nature of the result.

In the event of a non-runner in an accumulative bet, the non-runner is ignored and the bet stands on the lesser number of legs. A fourfold, for example, with one non-runner becomes a treble; a fourfold with two non-runners becomes a double.

Accumulative bets are extremely appealing to the betting public because they seem to offer the prospect of big payouts for small stakes. But, in life, one rarely gets anything for nothing!

How to calculate accumulative odds

Let us suppose a treble landing the following odds: 7/2, 13/8, and 10/11.

(1) Convert all the odds to odds-to-1 by dividing each lefthand figure by its righthand figure: 3.5/1, 1.625/1, and 0.909/1.

(2) Add 1 point to each new lefthand figure, ignore the righthand figure (1), and multiply: $4.5 \times 2.625 \times 1.909 = 22.55$

(3) Deduct 1 point to give the accumulative odds-to-1: 21.55/1.

A £1 bet at those odds would return £22.55 (21.55 winnings+£1 stake).

In reality, the stakes involved may be quite substantial – simply because winning returns, from successful legs, are automatically ploughed back into further bets rather than being tucked away in the bettor's savings account, so increasing the bettor's average investment over the whole bet quite dramatically.

That is why, for the bookmaker, accumulative bets are a very profitable form of business. In the early days of bookmaking, in the 19th century, vast fortunes were made out of laying 'double' prices, at a time when accumulative odds were not very well understood. Today we are much better informed but accumulative betting is just as popular!

See Multiple bets, Staking plans

Across-the-card

Term indicating bets on races at the same time at different meetings.

Some bookmakers (mainly smaller ones) apply special 'across-the-card' limits to accumulative bets involving successful selections in races run at or about the same time.

Action

The sum of the stakes of all the bets in a series (*ie* the bettor's turnover).

Since, in a given series, a bettor's action may be made up of recycled winnings as well as new money, it is evident that an amount of betting capital may finance action several times greater than itself.

All up to win

Phrase signifying that the place stake of an each-way wager will be added to the win stake in cases where there are too few runners for place betting.

See Each-way

All-ways

'All-ways' is a term used in forecast and tricast (or trio) betting to request all the possible alternative ways of arranging a given number of selections. For example, an 'all-ways forecast ABC' consists of 6 bets AB, AC, BA, BC, CA, CB – with the assurance that, provided 2 of the selections finish 1st and 2nd in the race, there is a winning bet.

The bettor should be careful to stake the correct number of

alternatives. If the slip is understaked, the bookmaker has special rules for apportioning the total money staked on the slip. In the case of overstaking, the excess is normally returnable to the bettor.

Tables of permutations are given on pages 42 and 118.

'All-ways' is the term usually used when making a full-cover forecast or trio bet on a greyhound track totalisator.

See Full-cover, Overstaking, Permutation, Understaking

Also ran

Phrase signifying an unplaced runner.

American football

All the main British bookmakers accept bets on NFL (National Football League) American football. There are also several 'independent' firms with a speciality interest in the sport.

Throughout the season, bookmakers offer odds for the Super Bowl, divisional and conference championships, and individual matches. Because many matches have an obvious favourite, handicap betting, whereby the lesser-favoured team ('underdog') is given a number of points' start, is the norm. This is known as the 'pointspread' or 'spread' and, from the bettor's point of view, the winner is not the team with the higher score but the one which 'covers the spread': in the case of the favourite, wins by a margin of points greater than the handicap points conceded; in the case of the underdog, wins 'straight-up' or loses by a margin less than the number of points received.

In Britain, handicap points are usually given to half-points (*eg* $3\frac{1}{2}$, $10\frac{1}{2}$, $14\frac{1}{2}$). This automatically rules out drawn results. In betting in the United States, a tied result is a 'push', stakes being returned to bettors. The aim of the bookmaker's oddsmaker, when determining the spread, is to equalise the demand for bets for the two teams, enabling the same odds (usually 10/11) to be offered for each. In the United States imbalanced demand is corrected by modifying the spread. British bookmakers usually prefer to change the odds (offering say 4/5 for one team, 1/1 the other) while leaving the spread unchanged. There is sometimes considerable disparity in spreads from one bookmaker to another, so the bettor should take the trouble to find the most favourable terms.

Some bookmakers insist on a minimum of trebles for regular season matches but the more adventurous are now offering singles.

If a match is tied after the normal 60 minutes' play (in practice, games go on much longer, the clock being stopped for interruptions), extra time (called 'overtime') is played. The first team to score in overtime prevails. It is important for the British bettor, accustomed to wagering on soccer, to note that in American football overtime *does* count for betting purposes.

The extra half-points can be deceptive: $3\frac{1}{2}$ points need two field goals or a touchdown to be covered.

As in soccer, home sides enjoy an advantage and some experts, in making their own handicap, award home teams 3 notional points to take account of this.

Due to the intensely physical nature of the sport, hard matches take their toll and may weaken a side for its next game. Weather conditions and motivation (so-called 'grudge' and 'revenge' factors) are reckoned to influence outcomes.

An article about American football from a betting point of view ('How to beat the American football "spread"' by Bryan Pugh) appears in 'The Sporting Life Guide to How to Pick Winners' (see p. 127).

Ante-post

Ante-post bets are wagers struck before the day of the event (in horse racing, up to 10.00am on the day prior to the race). The word 'post' has nothing to do with the 'starting post'. The post in question is the 'betting post' which, over 100 years ago, was a stake stuck in the ground at a racecourse as a rendezvous for those wishing to bet.

Ante-post betting is limited in the main to major events involving top-class contenders.

Except where a runner is 'balloted out', to limit the size of a field, ante-post bets are 'all-in run-or-not, entered-or-not'. That is to say, if a bet is struck on a selection which does not take part, the stake is forfeited. This is an important difference from 'day-of-the-race' or 'starting price' bets where wagers on non-runners are void with stakes returnable. (The 'all-in run-or-not' rule does not always apply to non-racing sports. Check the conditions before betting!)

There are therefore two gambles in an ante-post bet: one, a gamble on whether the runner will go to the start and, two, a gamble on whether it will succeed in the race. Since many unknown factors are involved, in particular those concerning the physical well-being of the selection, there is clearly a large element of luck in ante-post wagering which the bettor trades, in theory, for higher odds, although it by no means follows that the ante-post price will be greater than the price on the day. Clearly, it cannot make sense to take short odds about a runner in an ante-post book.

Ante-post prices vary from bookmaker to bookmaker, so would-

The betting post, about 1789

be bettors should shop around for the best on offer.

Ante-post bets on a race which does not take place are void, with stakes returnable. In the case of a postponement, bets stand until the event either takes place or is abandoned.

In the case of each-way bets at ante-post odds, the place terms are those applying at the time of making the bet, even if the field, on the day, is reduced to fewer than the number normally qualifying for place terms.

Where the same runner is backed to win both or all the legs of an ante-post double or treble, the advertised single odds apply only to the first leg. The bookmaker will necessarily lay different odds for the subsequent legs since these are related contingencies (see 'Related Contingencies', p. 90).

Ante-post wagers are mainly struck off-course but the on-course representatives of major firms are also able to lay ante-post wagers, free of Betting Duty.

See Hedging

Any-to-come

An instruction to re-invest all or part of a winning return on another bet. The term 'if-cash' is also sometimes used.

As 'any-to-come' bets are technically separate wagers, they become individually liable for tax (except in the case of 'any-to-come all on' which may be regarded as an accumulative bet), even if tax was prepaid on the original bet.

Away bookmaker

Racecourse bookmaker making a book on the day's racing at a meeting other than the one he is attending. Board or starting price terms are available.

See Home bookmaker

BAGS

Bookmakers' Afternoon Greyhound Services Ltd (BAGS) is a bookmakers' organisation (founded in 1967), which negotiates contracts with track promoters to provide the daytime greyhound racing service to betting shops.

The daytime greyhound service was originally conceived as insurance against lost betting turnover resulting from cancelled horse racing, but the popularity of greyhound racing as a wagering medium for betting shop clients has increased phenomenally and greyhound racing is now an important feature of the daytime betting shop service in its own right.

The number of meetings covered has increased year on year. At its inception, there were approximately 200 BAGS meetings. In 1991–92, 675 meetings were scheduled. One track, Hackney in London, operates exclusively on the BAGS service, most of its meetings being transmitted as live pictures as well as on the audio service, enabling greyhound enthusiasts everywhere the possibility of following the action from the track in its entirety.

Address: Bookmakers' Afternoon Greyhound Services Ltd, Francis House, Francis Street, London SW1P 1DE. Telephone: 071-630 0241.

See Greyhound betting

Banker

Selection regarded (hopefully) by the bettor as a near-certainty, used to lessen the cost of a permutation by reducing the number of bets required. Bettors who aspire to better-than-average performance should look for 'value' in their bankers as in all other selections.

Bar

A term used in betting shop broadcasts, to signify those runners in a race for which a price is not quoted. For example, '20/1 bar 9' would mean that a price of at least 20/1 is available against any runner other than the 9 already quoted. Betting shops do not usually lay bar prices.

Betting forecast

Odds predictions for the day's racing printed below the lists of runners in daily newpapers.

Betting-in-running

Racecourse bookmakers sometimes offer odds about a given runner or runners after a race is under way. When a bettor takes such odds, there is said to have been a bet-in-running. The bookmaker knows from experience and practice the situations where it is favourable from his own point of view so to do and he has the advantage of the initiative. It is a 'take it or leave it' situation and the racegoer, having little time to consider, is liable to be entrapped in an impulsive and unwise bet.

Another more genuine kind of betting-in-running, where the bettor usually has the opportunity of choosing from all the options, involves wagering on sports contests, such as golf, darts, snooker, football and so on, where the action unfolds over a long period of time and where sudden shifts in the fortunes of the contenders can drastically alter the probabilities. The increasing readiness of bookmaking firms to bet-in-running on sports contests has gone hand in hand with the availability of betting facilities at non-racing sports venues.

Bets-in-running may also be available to telephone clients on high-profile televised sporting events (during the closing stages of a major golf tournament, for example) and, to a more limited extent, to betting shop customers where details of offers-in-running (such as half-time odds on an important football match) may be announced on the audio service and displayed on information screens.

Betting market

The 'betting market' is made by the action in the main ring of a racecourse or greyhound track, where the odds on offer about different contenders fluctuate according to the demand for bets. The odds on offer around the time of the 'off' determine the 'starting prices' (SP), which form the basis of settlement of most off-course bets.

Leading off-course bookmaking companies have representatives at race meetings to bet on their behalf, either to lay-off liability or to make selective bets to remove distortions from the on-course market if it appears to be unrepresentative of betting patterns off-course. So long as the shortening of one price leads, as it should, to the lengthening of another, or others, the practice is not prejudicial to the interests of the betting public as a whole. The stated aim of off-course bookmaking firms is to balance their liabilities, not back winners or affect margins.

Many of those who object most strongly to such intervention are the keenest to have the traditional starting price system preserved. But they cannot have it all ways. Without a mechanism whereby off-course betting activity can communicate with the action in the Ring, the present system of starting price betting would probably become unworkable.

See Starting prices

Betting Office Licensees Association (BOLA)

Principal body representing the interests of betting shop licensees. It was founded (in 1973) by the then 'Big Four' betting shop companies but membership is open to all betting shop firms whatever their size.

Address: Betting Office Licensees Association, Francis House, Francis Street, London SW1P 1DE. Telephone: 071-630 0667.

Betting shops

Betting shops are not a modern creation. They first appeared in the 19th century, developing out of cigar shops, barbers and the like where bets were taken, at first, as a sideline. The 'invention' of cash betting (traditionally, wagering on horse racing had been based on credit, bettors holding their own stakes) enfranchised a new class of paying-up-front bettor, that is to say the ordinary man and woman. This resulted in a betting shop boom in the 1840's and early 1850's. Around 1850, there were reckoned to be some 300 betting shops in London alone, not including public houses and other premises where bets were taken as a sideline.

Unfortunately, there was a dark side to this democratic explosion in the form of several notorious cases of betting shop proprietors absconding. In response to anti-gambling lobbyists, the government of the day panicked. Instead of introducing legislation to regulate off-course betting, they rushed through a bill, in 1853, outlawing off-course cash betting.

Quashing betting shops did not suppress the public's desire to bet on horse races nor did it stop bookmakers from taking cash bets (although they risked fines and imprisonment). In particular, certain public houses became well-known as places where such wagers could be placed. This illegal trade in bets is vividly portrayed in the novel *Esther Waters* by George Moore (1894).

Cash betting shops remained illegal for over 100 years. The persistent flouting of the law caused an uneasy accommodation to develop between law-enforcers and law-breakers, and inevitably corrupt advantage was taken of the situation.

In the 20th century, the development of the telephone system and wire services gave an added immediacy to off-course betting. Town centre 'credit offices' began to appear. Such offices were credit in name only, operating in a manner not unlike a modern betting shop, although they were permeated by a somewhat furtive atmosphere and the walls were plastered with notices stating that loitering was not allowed and that only credit bets would be taken!

By the time the law legalising betting shops came into force, in 1961, there was already an infrastructure of cash betting outlets in existence. The good news of lawful cash betting off-course was shortly followed, in 1966, by the bad news of the imposition of Betting Duty on all off-course bets.

Today there are around 9,500 betting shops in the UK. The so-called 'Big Three' (Ladbrokes, William Hill and Corals) own around 42% of the outlets, generating about 60% of total annual off-course betting turnover.

Under the law as it stands, betting shops are obliged to close at the latest at 6.30pm. However, the possibility of a relaxation of the law to permit evening opening is presently a matter of discussion. It is an issue on which opinion is deeply divided.

Persons under 18 are disallowed by law from entering betting shops.

Bias

Racecourses and sports grounds have 'form' as well as runners and players. Perhaps the most recognised example of this phenomenon is home-ground advantage, which strongly biases football matches to the 'home' result.

In horse racing, the variable nature of courses sometimes favours one side over another. Advice on likely 'draw advantage' is given with the day's racing details in *The Sporting Life*.

In greyhound racing, in very wet conditions, one side of the track (usually the outside) may run faster than the other, improving the chances of the runners on that side. Weather conditions may also be responsible for reducing contests to raw luck. A gluey playing surface and slippery ball may effectively equalise the chances of two otherwise unequal teams.

To bet in defiance of obviously biased conditions can be disastrous. At the same time, bettors are cautioned against seeing bias where none may exist. Several winners from one trap during an afternoon's dog racing, for example, may be no more than mere coincidence.

Board price

Another term for 'show price'. In modernised betting shops, the practice of marking betting shows from the course on lists of runners fixed to a board has been superseded by displays on television screens.

See Show price

Bonuses and consolations

Many speciality bets (*ie* 'own-name' multiple bets on special printed slips) incorporate bonus and consolation dividends. Offers (*eg* 'guaranteed minimum forecasts' and 'boosted' SPs for long-priced winners) may also be made during racing on the betting shop broadcast (major firms operate their own commentaries).

Bettors should be wary since the purpose of such offers may be to divert custom in the direction of the most profitable (for the bookmaker) forms of business – outsiders, multiple bets at hard-to-land long odds and computer forecasts. However, offers are increasingly being used by bookmakers to compete with one another for business. Bettors should look for and obtain the most advantageous terms for the bet of their choice.

Bookmaker

Although the term has come to be applied to all persons or firms authorised to take bets from the public, on- or off-course, a bookmaker, strictly speaking, is one who makes a market in bets, offering and adjusting odds for the different runners in response to demand. The term dates from the early days of the craft when the notebook and pencil conspicuously carried for recording bets, as and when they were taken, was an identifying mark of the professional betting man.

Although betting shop firms may 'make' ante-post 'books' on special events, most of their trade is 'starting price' business – that is to say, settled at odds based on prices determined by the real market-makers, the bookmakers at the course.

How do bookmakers at the course operate the betting market, and so indirectly determine the odds at which most off-course bets are settled?

The 'first show' is based on what are known as the 'tissue' odds, worked out before the meeting by an expert in 'form'. Although these prices reflect the chances of the runners, the opening odds are really a stab at guessing the proportions in which the public will want to bet. But, because the public is also influenced by what the bookmakers do, the battle is partly won by this first show of prices!

Bookmakers mark up the opening odds in a fairly circumspect way to allow room for whatever corrective changes – sometimes minor, sometimes quite drastic – which may become necessary to adjust their liabilities as a result of the actual demand for bets.

The first show, therefore, is usually very over-round (see 'Odds', p. 69) and, unless the bettor has reason to believe the bookmakers are laying palpably mistaken odds which could quickly disappear, this is not a good time to make a bet. In order to get betting under way, the bookmaker has to start a process of general relaxation, so that a 'book' is usually least over-round at the time of the 'off'.

The large bookmaking concerns have representatives at the tracks who can make selective bets to lay-off liability or to influence the odds if the market formed seems prejudicial to their interest. The object of such intervention is to remove distortions from the on-course market, making it more representative of the pattern of staking off-course. It is not necessarily prejudicial to the interest of the individual bettor, since a cut in one price is usually followed by a relaxation in the prices of other runners.

Bookmakers do not necessarily always try to balance their books. Many course bookmakers like to gamble (from a position of strength, of course!) so that sometimes, if the bookmaker is personally convinced a fancied runner has little chance, he may offer a price above the going odds in order to attract what he hopes will be profitable business. Queues of eager bettors quickly gather round his pitch anxious to obtain the favourable odds. Sometimes the bookmaker is successful, in which case he goes home with his bag bulging more than usual. Other times, the gamble fails and, when the time comes to pay out, there is a line of smug clients waiting to empty his satchel.

See Betting market, Odds, Racecourse betting

Canadian

See Super Yankee

Carry-forward pool

Totalisator bet in which unwon sums are carried forward from one meeting to another. The Tote Jackpot and Placepot are examples. Many greyhound tracks also feature carry-forward pools.

When a pool has a carried-forward element, the value to the bettor is enhanced by virtue of the fact that the carried-forward sum is a valuable bonus payment to which the bettor participating on that one day has not contributed.

Chance

A 'chance' is an outcome which is possible but uncertain. For example, of throwing a 'six' with a die, of Labour (or Conservatives) winning most seats in a General Election, of Manchester United winning the League championship and so on. The likelihood of any given chance is its 'probability'.

In trying to understand a sport or other form of contest from a betting point of view, it is important to analyse from where and how the uncertainty arises. In most sporting events, outcomes are determined partly by factors known to the observer and partly by factors known only to nature. The more that is known by the observer and the less known exclusively to nature, the more predictable the outcome. Lack of trial or race form, the shuffling effect of occurrences in the course of a race (falling in National Hunt racing or incidents of crowding or bumping during a greyhound race), or the shuffling of known abilities in the process known as handicapping are various ways which contribute to the ratio of unknowable to knowable.

Some bettors are apt to underestimate the role of the factors known only to nature, and therefore are liable to attach unwarranted conviction to their predictions.

See Probability

Chart

Literally a chart, published by the National Sporting League (a bookmakers' organisation), for the possible combinations of starting prices of the first and second finishers in a race.

It is used to determine the return (inclusive of stake), to a £1 unit, on off-course forecast bets where a 'computer forecast' is not declared – for evening greyhounds, for example. The Chart dividends include an element for tax, so are not liable to any deduction.

Chart forecast dividends are given, when appropriate, in the results published in the press.

See Forecast

Computer forecast

The 'computer straight forecast' (horse racing) and 'BAGS computer forecast' (greyhounds) – the basis on which most betting shop forecasts are settled. The dividends are largely determined by the starting prices returned for the race.

Computer forecasts include an element of tax. Therefore, no tax should be added to a forecast bet. Nor is there any deduction from the return. The dividends are returned to a £1 unit and are deemed to be inclusive of stake.

For specified horse races (handicaps of 8 or more declared runners and no fewer than 6 actual runners) and BAGS greyhound races of 6 runners or more there is also a 'computer tricast' dividend.
See Chart, Forecast, Tricast

Conditional bet

A wager which is dependent on the fulfilment of a certain condition. For example, 'any-to-come' (or 'if-cash') bets, 'if win' or 'if lose' bets, and 'stop-at-a-winner'.

Contingency

Event which determines the outcome of a bet – crossing a line first, scoring most points, winning most parliamentary seats, and so on.
See Related contingencies

Coup

A coup (pronounced 'koo') is a French word, meaning 'blow' or 'cut', absorbed into English to signify a successful move or stroke. In racing, a coup is a successful bet, or bets, landed at long odds by a runner's connections as a result of covert manoeuvring designed to ensure that, when the runner in question is entered for a race which it is likely to be able to win easily, its ability will be greatly underestimated by bookmakers and public.

Occasionally, coups have been attempted which have been blatantly fraudulent. But coups can be, and are, mounted without infringing either law or rules of racing. However, a question of probity is raised since the benefits that accrue to the organisers of the coup are at the expense of the betting public as a whole who, in ignorance of what is afoot, have staked their money, in good faith, on what is apparent purely on the evidence of the formbook.
See Gamble, Rigged betting

Coupling

In some countries overseas, horses in the same ownership running in the same race are 'coupled' for betting purposes. Thus, in French racing, the backer of a coupled horse is on both (or all) horses in the same ownership for one stake. The coupling applies to win bets or the win part of each-way bets only.

Course-to-course

Course-to-course betting is a Tote facility whereby racegoers at one meeting are able to bet into the pools at other meetings. Introduced in February 1991, at first at selected meetings, it is planned to accommodate up to five meetings on any one day when the system is fully operational.

See Tote betting, on-course

Cover to win

A wager in which a selection is backed to win a specified sum, the stake depending on the starting price. For practical reasons, such bets are not normally accepted by cash betting shops but may be available from some firms to credit clients.

Cover to win £100 ready reckoner					
1/5	500.00	evens	100.00	5/1	20.00
2/9	450.00	21/20	95.24	11/2	18.18
1/4	400.00	11/10	90.91	6/1	16.67
2/7	350.00	6/5	83.33	13/2	15.38
30/100	333.33	5/4	80.00	7/1	14.29
1/3	300.00	11/8	72.73	15/2	13.33
4/11	275.00	6/4	66.67	8/1	12.50
2/5	250.00	13/8	61.54	17/2	11.76
4/9	225.00	7/4	57.14	9/1	11.11
40/85	212.50	15/8	53.33	10/1	10.00
1/2	200.00	2/1	50.00	11/1	9.09
8/15	187.50	85/40	47.06	12/1	8.33
4/7	175.00	9/4	44.44	14/1	7.14
8/13	162.50	5/2	40.00	16/1	6.25
4/6	150.00	11/4	36.36	18/1	5.56
8/11	137.50	3/1	33.33	20/1	5.00
4/5	125.00	100/30	30.00	25/1	4.00
5/6	120.00	7/2	28.57	33/1	3.03
10/11	110.00	4/1	25.00	40/1	2.50
20/21	105.00	9/2	22.22	50/1	2.00

Credit accounts

Credit accounts, enabling bets to be made by telephone, can be opened, subject to approved references, with specialist credit firms and most leading bookmakers.

See Deposit accounts, Direct debit betting

Cross bet

A 'single-stakes-about' bet. So-called because it is customary to indicate the bet with a cross or series of crosses between the selections.

See Single-stakes-about

Day-of-the-race price

Special early odds laid by bookmakers on the day of the race prior to the formation of a betting market on the course.

Such prices are publicised through advertisements in the daily sporting press, on screen displays and on lists of runners in betting shops. Unlike ante-post prices, bets on non-runners are void with stakes returnable. However, in the event of a withdrawal, such day-of-the-race prices are subject to the Rule 4c scale of deductions (horse racing) or are settled at starting prices (greyhounds).

Day-of-the-race prices are subject to fluctuation, depending on demand.

See Ante-post, Early prices, Tattersalls Rule 4c

Dead-heat

A result in which two or more competitors reach the winning line at the same time.

In a dead-heat for first place, bets are settled by dividing the stake by the number of runners involved in the dead-heat and paying full odds to the divided stake, the rest of the stake being lost. Place bets are settled in a similar manner at the appropriate odds where more than the required number of runners are placed.

Deposit accounts

Deposit betting facilities, for those wishing to bet by telephone without being involved in credit, are available from most leading bookmaking firms.

An agreed sum is deposited with the bookmaker and the bettor, using a personalised account number, can bet by telephone up to his available balance.

See Credit accounts, Direct debit betting

Direct debit betting

Direct debit cards ('Switch' or 'Delta'), issued by many leading banks and building societies, are a comparatively new way of paying for goods and services. When a debit card is used, payment is made, as with a cheque, by directly debiting the bank or building society account of the card-holder. Most leading bookmakers accept bets by telephone using debit cards. Winning returns are likewise directly *credited* to the card-holder's bank account.

Debit card bets are subject to a minimum total investment per call, typically £10.

Disputes

The ultimate arbitrator in horse racing betting disputes is Tattersalls Committee. Address: The Secretary, Tattersalls Committee, PO Box 13, 19 Wilwyne Close, Caversham, Reading RG4 0XZ.

At the races, a Ring Inspector is available to investigate the circumstances of disputes between bettors and bookmakers, help resolve the situation and, if necessary, advise the parties of their right to refer the matter to Tattersalls Committee. Many racecourse bookmakers tape-record bets which provides a means of checking the instructions given and taken where these are disputed.

The 'Green Seal Service' is a betting arbitration service provided by *The Sporting Life*, renowned for its impartial and authoritative opinions on betting matters. Write to: Green Seal Service, The Sporting Life, Orbit House, 1 New Fetter Lane, London EC4A 1AR (please enclose an SAE).

Many betting shop firms incorporate in their rules a provision whereby disputes which cannot be resolved between the parties should be referred either to Tattersalls (for horse racing) or to an arbitrator nominated by the Editor of *The Sporting Life*.

See Green Seal Service, Ring Inspector, Tattersalls Committee

Double

Bet involving 2 selections, in different events, in which the total return from the first selection (stake+winnings) is automatically staked on the second selection. Both selections must succeed for the bet to pay a return.

Double-stakes-about (D-S-A)

A bet consisting of 2 singles, each with an 'any-to-come' single at twice the original stake on the other selection. In effect, this trebles the stake on each selection if both win. Thus:

> 50p A any-to-come £1 B
> 50p B any-to-come £1 A

The any-to-come bets are technically separate wagers, so that, even if tax has been prepaid on the original bets, further tax is due on any return arising from the any-to-come elements of the bet.

If this bet is required, it should be marked 'double-stakes-about' or 'D-S-A'. A cross or series of crosses between the selections only indicates 'stakes-about' and, unless stated otherwise, will be taken to mean 'single-stakes-about'.

See Single-stakes-about, Stakes-about

Doubly-engaged

A doubly-engaged horse is one which is entered for two races on the same day.

Where a time is given, the bet holds only for the race for which it is timed. In the other race, it will be treated as a non-runner. If the bettor wishes to be on the horse wherever it runs, it should not be timed.

Down-the-card

Indicates races at the same meeting (with different off-times), differentiating from 'across-the-card' meaning races at different meetings with the same or similar off-times.

Dual-forecast

The equivalent of a 'reverse forecast' for a single stake. Two runners are nominated and the bet wins if the selections finish 1st and 2nd in either order.

The Tote offers a dual-forecast at racecourses, also available off-course from Tote Bookmakers and bookmakers licensed to bet at Tote odds. In the event of the Tote dividend not being declared on the 1st and 2nd placed horses, off-course Tote dual-forecast bets coupling the two successful horses are settled as a reverse computer forecast with the stake divided.

To combine several selections in one race as dual-forecasts, the following are the number of bets required:

2 selections	1 bet
3 selections	3 bets
4 selections	6 bets
5 selections	10 bets
6 selections	15 bets

Each-way

An 'each-way' bet is a win and place bet. There are two stakes: one for the win part, the other for the place part. If the selection finishes 1st, both win and place bets pay a return. The win bet returns the win stake and full odds. The place bet returns the place stake and a proportion of the win odds (see table on facing page).

If the selection fails to win but is placed, the win bet fails and the win stake is lost. But the place bet pays a return and, of course, the place stake is returned.

Place-only bets are not normally accepted in betting shops.

Conditions for each-way betting vary according to circumstances. The table illustrates usual terms:

Horse and greyhound racing		
2–4 runners	No place betting (all up to win)	
5–7 runners	1–2	One-quarter odds
8+ runners	1–2–3	One-fifth odds
Horse racing handicaps		
12–15 runners	1–2–3	One-quarter odds
16+ runners	1–2–3–4	One-quarter odds

In Tote or pari-mutuel betting, the place part of an each-way bet is not a proportion of the win odds but the place pool dividend.

Psychologically, many bettors look to the place part of their each-way bets as insurance for their win bets. Such each-way bettors may therefore be drawn to wagers at odds of about 5/1 and more, a region of the odds which statistically bears a heavier burden of over-round (see 'Odds', p. 69) than the runners at shorter odds, where horse race bettors are more likely to find value (see p. 122).
See Equally-divided

Each-way all each-way

See Equally-divided

Early prices

Many firms offer prices throughout the day on selected horse and greyhound races to be run later. Such odds are, of course, subject to fluctuation and are usually available up to a stated interval before the race or until the first show from the course, whichever is first.

If the bettor wishes to strike his bet at an early price in preference to the starting price, the counter clerk must be asked to note and initial the odds on the betting slip.

Bets on non-runners are void with stakes returnable but, in such cases, horse race bets on the remaining runners are subject to Rule 4c and greyhound bets revert to SP.
See Tattersalls Rule 4c

Edge

Arithmetical advantage of the bookmaker, totalisator or promoter of a gambling game over the player. Expressed as a percentage, the 'edge' is the number of pounds the promoter can expect to gain from every £100 wagered. The term is more commonly associated with casino games – as in 'house edge' – than with sports betting where it is more usual to speak of the bookmaker's advantage in terms of 'over-round'. A 'book' which is 120 over-round is equivalent to an edge of 16.7% (20/120ths). A totalisator's edge is the percentage retention from the pool.

In a game devoid of skill (such as the casino game of roulette), all players (making the same class of bet), over the long term contribute equally (in proportion to amount wagered) to the promoter's edge. In gambling situations where skill plays a part, as in the casino game of blackjack and in most sports betting, better-than-average play means a smaller contribution to the promoter's edge while worse-than-average play results in a greater contribution.

Election betting

See Political betting

Equally-divided (ED)

A method of settling each-way bets in doubles, trebles and accumulators in which the total return from one leg is divided into two equal parts for the win and place stake of the next leg.

Win-to-win and place-to-place settlement is more usual but most bookmakers will apply equally-divided settlement if this is requested on the betting slip, except in the case of speciality bets.

Equally-divided is also known as 'each-way all each-way'.

Evening racing

Bets on major evening greyhound meetings and evening horse racing may be made off-course at betting shops. Such bets are settled at the official starting prices.

Much-reduced limits govern bets on evening racing. Any bettor contemplating a large stake or a bet which could land long odds (such as an accumulator or multiple bet) should first check the firm's rules for the appropriate limits to ensure that the terms are satisfactory.

Bets at some evening greyhound venues, mainly smaller ones where the betting market is considered too weak to guarantee the return of reliably representative odds, may not be accepted. Would-be bettors should consult the firm's rules for up-to-date details of acceptable tracks and the special limits governing payouts on evening greyhound racing.

Most firms accept all bets on greyhound 'open races', provided the racecard and result are published in *The Sporting Life*. However,

there may be exceptions, so the rules should be checked.
See Limits, Multiple bets, Open race

Evens

Terms of a wager in which bookmaker and bettor stake equal
amounts (1/1).
See Odds

Expectation

The 'mathematical expectation' is the amount a bettor would stand
to lose or gain over the long term if a bet of given odds and
probability were made repetitiously. In effect, it is a bet's 'value'.

Expectation is calculated by summing each possible gain or loss
multiplied by the probability of that gain or loss. Coin-spinning is of
questionable appeal as a candidate for a betting game but, by virtue
of its simplicity and the known probabilities of the two possible
outcomes, it is useful for illustrative purposes!

Let us suppose a wager of £1 at odds of 4/5 about 'heads':

Probability of gain	0.5 (50% = 50/100 = 0.5)
Amount of gain	£0.80 (4/5×£1)
Probability of loss	0.5 (50% = 50/100 = 0.5)
Amount of loss	−£1.00

Expectation = (0.5×£0.80)+(0.5×(−£1.00)) = −£0.10

In the short term, the bettor may experience untypical losses or
gains. But, over the long term, a bettor wagering on a 0.5 ('evens' or
50%) chance at odds of 4/5, as given in the example, can expect to
lose 10p of every £ wagered. The following are the expectations for
a 0.5 (50%) chance given different payout odds:

Odds	Expectation
4/5	−0.10
10/11	−0.045
1/1	0.0
11/10	+0.05
5/4	+0.125

A bet in which the expectation is 0 is said to be a 'fair bet'.

Different amounts staked, on bets of the same odds and
probability, have different expectations – *in money terms*. But,
expressed as a *percentage* of the amount staked, expectation is
always the same. It follows that a series of bets of the same
probability at the same odds, taken together, has the same
percentage expectation as each component bet, even if, from
occasion to occasion, different amounts are wagered. Let us
imagine the unlikely taker of 'heads' at odds of 4/5 and a

progression of 3 bets in which the stake is doubled each time: £1, £2, £3. The sum of the expectations is:

$$(-10p/\pounds1)+(-20p/\pounds2)+(-30p/\pounds3)=-60p/\pounds6$$

The expectation of the series is therefore −10% ((−.60/6.00)×100), as it is for each component bet. No amount of varying of sums wagered can therefore turn this, or any other, series of bets, each with a negative expectation, into a series of bets with an expectation other than a negative one. This is why so-called 'staking plans' do not work (see p. 103).

If a series of bets consists of bets each with a different but *unknown* expectation, then the expectation of the series stands for the expectation of each component bet. If such a series has a negative expectation, then each component bet is considered to have a negative expectation.

Unlike coin-spinning, where the probabilities of the outcomes can be known more or less exactly, estimates of the chances of the contenders in sporting events, which always involve many unknowable factors, are conjectures with a wide latitude of error. Expectation calculations based on such guesses would necessarily be extremely hypothetical. However, expectation calculations are legitimately and usefully applicable in racing and sports betting to obtain average values in statistical contexts. Also, an understanding of expectation is essential for obtaining insight into all forms of betting from a mathematical point of view.

See Probability, Value

Face

A racecourse bookmakers' colloquialism for the antithesis of a 'mug punter' – a bettor who commands respect, not by virtue of the amount wagered ('mugs' know no limit to the size of their bets), but because the 'face' is believed to be in possession of useful knowledge. 'Betting to faces' refers to the practice of hedging the face's selection while laying other runners liberally.

See Mug

Fair bet

A 'fair bet' is one which, if repeated on the same terms over the long term, would result in losses roughly balancing winnings. The bettor making such a bet would therefore have neither an advantage nor a disadvantage. Such a bet has a 'mathematical expectation' of zero.

A wager at 1/1 ('evens') for a proposition with 0.5 probability (50% chance) of success, such as 'heads' (or 'tails') in a coin-spinning game, would be a fair bet.

See Expectation, Favourable game, Unfavourable game

Favourable game

A 'favourable game' is a mathematical term for a betting proposition in which a player has a positive expectation. In commercially promoted games, such as those played in casinos or racing and sports betting, the games are (naturally enough!) favourable, overall, to the promoter, although on individual occasions in games involving skill there may be situations favourable to the bettor.

In games involving skill, advantages to the bettor arising from skilful play are usually more than balanced by a greater rate of gain to the promoter arising from the bets of unskilled players. That is why it can actually pay casinos to promote a game of skill such as blackjack.

Games devoid of skill, such as roulette, are favourable to the promoter alone. The search for a profitable roulette system is quite futile. The player's expectation (for the same class of bet) is the same – a negative one – on every spin of the wheel, regardless of what numbers have gone before and regardless of what fluctuations of fortune have been experienced by the player.

A game where the player's expectation is negative is known as 'unfavourable'. A game which is neither favourable nor unfavourable – such as coin-spinning with an evens payout – is said to be 'fair'.

See Expectation, Fair bet, Unfavourable game

Favourite

The 'favourite' is the runner at the lowest odds and, in theory, the one supported by the greatest weight of money.

Bettors who wish to bet on the favourite, whichever runner it turns out to be, may do so simply by specifying 'Favourite' on their betting slip, taking care to state meeting and time. All kinds of difficulty arise if meeting and time are omitted, so backers of unnamed favourites should take care to see that these details are given.

Most bookmakers will accept bets for unnamed 1st, 2nd and 3rd favourites in horse racing, and for unnamed 1st favourites in greyhound racing.

If two runners share favouritism, they are, for betting purposes, joint 1st and 2nd favourites. Backers of either the unnamed 1st or 2nd favourite have their stake divided with one-half invested in each. If there are 3 co-favourites, they are joint 1st, 2nd and 3rd favourites and, similarly, backers of unnamed 1st, 2nd and 3rd favourites have their stake divided with one-third invested in each.

When a favourite is withdrawn, not under orders, and Rule 4c applies, that horse remains the favourite for betting purposes. Backers of the unnamed favourite are therefore on a non-runner. There is an exception to this rule for certain speciality bets requiring a runner. The rules for substitution vary from firm to firm, so the interested bettor should consult his own betting shop's rule.

There are two points of interest about the favourite:

(1) A very high proportion of races are won by the market leader:

National Hunt (1986–91)	39.5%
Flat (1986–90)	36.2%
Greyhounds (graded races)	33.0% (approx)

(2) The bookmakers' margin of profit, overall, is less on favourites and other short-priced runners (and correspondingly more on outsiders). Generally-speaking, therefore, the bettor stands to lose less betting on shorter-priced runners. That is true of both horse and greyhound racing.

These are impressive facts, so much so that many bettors construct their entire betting strategy around the favourite – looking in particular for ways of perhaps making a profit by betting on some favourites and leaving others alone. The idea has been around a long time, even turning up in a 19th century novel (*Esther Waters* by George Moore):

> 'Are they outsiders he backs?'
> 'No, only favourites, [replied the bookmaker]. But what I can't make out is that there are times when he won't touch them; and when he don't, nine times out of ten they're beaten'.

Some categories of race are, in fact, more likely to be won by the favourite than others – non-handicap horse races and 'open' greyhound races, for example. That is because the form is more clear-cut, but favourites in such cases are afflicted by correspondingly cramped odds. Value may be difficult to find.

A more promising selective approach is to examine individual favourites on their merits and discard those which appear to have been promoted to the head of the market for a reason other than ability – sentiment, patriotic fervour, media hype, an appealing name, rumour and other such factors which sometimes strongly influence the public's choice.

See Value

Field

All the competitors in a race except the preferred one. Thus, for a bookmaker, it denotes all the runners other than the favourite. For a bettor, all the runners other than the selection, as, for example, in the instruction 'Trap 6 with the field'.

See With the field

Field money

Bookmakers' term for all the money staked by bettors for a given event.

First past the post

Mode of settling in which bets are paid out on the order of finish, regardless of any subsequent alteration of placings arising from an objection or stewards' enquiry. Betting shops settling by this method, mainly in the north and Scotland, will normally settle on the official result if the slip is marked 'RR' or 'racing rules'.

Bets such as forecasts which rely on dividends, however, are settled according to the official result.

Greyhound bets are always settled on the actual order of finish.

See Racing rules

First show

Opening sets of odds put up by the course bookmakers for an event. In a betting shop context, the first set of odds transmitted from the course.

See Odds

Fixed fraction betting

No form of staking plan can make a series of bets with a negative expectation into a positive one (see 'Expectation' on p. 32). Sooner or later, the bettor's capital will be exhausted and new funds required to continue. However, the bettor who wagers with a positive expectation will tend to reach a specified level of winnings at a faster rate if, instead of staking a fixed proportion of *starting* capital at each bet, he wagers a fixed proportion of *present* capital.

A bettor who decided to risk, say, one-twentieth of a starting capital of £200 would always stake a level £10. A bettor staking one-twentieth of present capital would only wager £10 if his capital stood at exactly £200. If his capital increased to, say, £250, the stake would be one-twentieth of that amount, *ie* £12.50. If his capital fell below £200 to, say, £190, the stake would be reduced in proportion to £9.50.

Since winnings do not necessarily come in round numbers, the bettor operating such a plan must necessarily, on occasions, also 'round' the amount staked. Thus, a bettor with a total capital of £279 would stake £14, or possibly £15, not £13.95. Rounding-over on one occasion is balanced by rounding-under on another, though it is in the interest of the bettor to operate as closely to the correct figure as possible without irritating the bookmaker taking the bet.

This method of betting has an interesting theoretical property. Since the bettor never wagers more than a given fraction of present capital, a balance of available capital always remains. The bettor, *in theory*, cannot be wiped out! In practice, of course, he can, because at a certain point the bookmaker's minimum stake is encountered and it is necessary to wager an amount greater than that prescribed.

Fixed fraction betting decrees changes in amounts staked in response to the bettor's present 'wealth' and not in response to any pattern of prior winning or losing bets. It is therefore excluded from the general criticism of betting plans where stakes are varied in response to antecedent events.

This method of betting is sometimes known as the 'Kelly system' after a mathematician who studied it.

See Expectation, Kelly system, Staking plans

Flag

A wager of 23 bets consisting of 4 selections (A,B,C,D) in a Yankee (11 bets) and single-stakes-about in pairs (12 bets). Thus: AB, AC, AD, BC, BD, CD, ABC, ABD, ACD, BCD, ABCD, A a-t-c B, B a-t-c A, A a-t-c C, C a-t-c A, A a-t-c D, D a-t-c A, B a-t-c C, C a-t-c B, B a-t-c D, D a-t-c B, C a-t-c D, D a-t-c C.

See Any-to-come

Football betting

Throughout the League season, most betting shops issue 'individual odds' coupons, for both midweek and weekend matches. These coupons are simple to fill out, give a wide range of bets and odds, and offer more realistic chances for success than football pools. Wins of up to £250,000 are possible on some coupons – with no pool sharing!

The potential payout of big accumulative bets should always be checked against the coupon limit, as this will reveal if the unit stake will take the bet through the ceiling. In which case, the stake should be scaled down or a bookmaker with a higher limit found. The coupon limits of smaller firms may, of course, be much less than those of the large companies. To avoid disappointment, the bettor should not wait for his lucky day to arrive before checking the rules!

As part of the agreement with the Football League for use of the copyright fixture list, bets involving League matches are limited to trebles and upwards (excepting matches broadcast live on UK TV on which singles are allowed). However, singles and doubles are available in the case of internationals, principal domestic cup competitions, and various European cup competitions. 'Correct score' bets are available in singles and upwards.

In the 'long list', most bookmakers limit bets involving any home selections to a minimum of a fivefold, although this rule is relaxed in the case of midweek coupons on which the minimum is a treble even with home selections. Many bettors find the fivefold minimum rule irksome and a few bookmakers have responded, either by dropping the fivefold restriction altogether or by allowing trebles on an abbreviated list consisting of the first two English divisions and the Scottish Premier division.

Bookmakers usually price up individual matches so that the 'percentage' is around 110 (an edge of 9%). However, the bettor can get a better deal by comparing the prices available from different firms. By betting selectively where the best odds are to be had, the bettor can greatly improve the terms on which he bets, effectively lowering the 'percentage' to about an average 106 (an edge of 5.7%).

Correct-score betting and double-result forecasts (halftime result and fulltime result) are popular with the football betting public but bettors should be aware that profit margins for the bookmakers may be 25% or more and about 15% respectively.

Coupons, including those for matches to be played on the following weekend, are usually available in the shops at the beginning of each week. Sunday and midweek results are not therefore assimilated into the following weekend's prices. Bookmakers can, and sometimes do, make changes to coupon prices after printing but, on the whole, are reluctant to do so because of the misunderstandings and bad will that can result. This enables bettors to profit from any form pointers arising from midweek results.

The following aspects of football betting sometimes give difficulty:

(1) Football bets are settled on 90 minutes' play, not the result after extra time – except in the case of special events (such as the Cup Final) when two sets of odds, for '90 minutes' and 'to win outright', may be offered. Where this option is given, bets are settled on 90 minutes unless 'to win outright' is stated on the slip. The referee is the arbiter of 90 minutes' play.

In the case of American football bets, on the other hand, overtime does count for betting purposes.

(2) Odds are sometimes offered for a number of contingencies in the same match – for example, first goalscorer, halftime result/fulltime result, and so on. Accumulative bets (doubles, trebles etc) on such related contingencies are not allowed (see 'Related contingencies', p. 90). Where such bets are taken in error, the stake is equally divided and invested as singles.

(3) 'First goal scorer' bets sometimes cause controversy, where the goal is claimed by (or given away to!) another player. Since 1985, *The Sporting Life* has declined to rule on the identification of first-scorers on the grounds that there are no 'official' goalscorers as, say, there are official results in horse racing. Nevertheless, the *Life* believes bookmakers should settle in accordance with the result sanctioned by the relevant football authority. 'Own goals' do not usually count in first-scorer betting. If a selected first-goal scorer does not play or comes on to the field as a substitute after the first-goal has been scored, the bettor's stake is returned.

(4) In the case of an abandoned match, bookmakers' rules may vary. Some rule, for example, that the score at the time of abandonment should stand as the result of the match. Others that only matches abandoned *after half-time* stand, earlier abandonments being void. Check the rules!

A sport in which around 30% of results are dead-heats is self-evidently an indecisive one. Although football fans may be loath to admit it, a high proportion of matches are decided by chance events – even the whim of a referee – rather than the relative merits of the two teams. The results of football matches, therefore, can often seem annoyingly perverse. As the prestigious scientific journal *Nature* commented at the time of the 1990 World Cup, the game as played at present yields scores too small to be regarded as an objective measure of the abilities of the two teams.

Nature suggested setting the goalposts wider apart, but, until that improbable reform is enacted by the football authorities, the football bettor is urged to base his betting policy around the statistical verities of the game, trimmed here and there, as necessary, by any salient information. Some of the most effective football betting campaigns have had a statistical basis. Bookmaking firms have progressively cut back odds on certain types of results, such as 'draws', where mathematically-minded bettors seemed to be getting the better of them.

As matters stand, the best value is probably to be found among the odds for home results. As such, the present restrictive rule, limiting 'homes' bettors to fivefolds and more, can be seen as a force that encourages bettors towards areas of betting (*ie* 'draws' and 'aways') which are more profitable business for the bookmakers.

An article about football from a betting point of view by *Sporting Life* expert Derrick Shaw appears in 'The Sporting Life Guide to How to Pick Winners' (see p. 127).

See Related contingencies

Forecast

Bet in which the requirement is to nominate, in correct order, the runners to finish 1st and 2nd in a race.

To nominate 2 runners in either order (a 'reverse forecast'), the bettor must make 2 bets. This is a simple form of 'permutation'. Other permutations giving even more cover may be selected. For example, 3 runners may be selected to be combined all-ways. This comprises 6 bets, the bettor being on a winner if the first and second finishers come from the 3 selections.

Like 'win' bets, forecasts may be combined in doubles and trebles. Forecast doubles are especially popular with followers of greyhound racing. For this purpose, many shops supply special printed slips, making such bets easier to write and helping to avoid staking errors.

The attraction of forecast doubles and trebles is the possibility of

Forecast doubles

No. of races	Naming, in each race, two to finish 1st and 2nd in correct order	Naming, in each race, two to finish 1st and 2nd in either order	Naming three in each race, any two of which to finish 1st and 2nd
2	1	4	36
3	3	12	108
4	6	24	216
5	10	40	360
6	15	60	540
7	21	84	756
8	28	112	1008
9	36	144	1296
10	45	180	1620
11	55	220	1980
12	66	264	2376

Forecast trebles

No. of races	Straight forecast trebles (2 selections in written order)	Reversed forecast trebles (2 selections in either order)
3	1	8
4	4	32
5	10	80
6	20	160
7	35	280
8	56	448
9	84	672
10	120	960
11	165	1320
12	220	1760

For dual-forecast trebles guide, see 'Triesta' on p. 118

Dual-forecasts and straight forecasts
No. of bets required to combine several selections in one race all-ways

No. of selections	Dual-forecasts	Straight forecasts
2	1	2
3	3	6
4	6	12
5	10	20
6	15	30

a very substantial win for a small stake, although the long odds must necessarily make success correspondingly more remote. Some firms allow forecasts to be combined in Patents or even Yankees. Look for the special printed slips.

Winning betting shop forecast bets are settled in accordance with the CSF (computer straight forecast) dividend (horse racing), the BAGS computer forecast dividend (daytime greyhound racing) or, in circumstances where there is no computer forecast (evening greyhound racing, for example), the Chart forecast dividend. These dividends are declared to a £1 unit stake and published, as appropriate, with the race results in the press. There is an allowance for tax in the dividend, so no extra should be added to a forecast stake. Nor is there any deduction from the return.

Betting shop greyhound 'dividends' should not be confused with the dividends paid to racegoers at the track. Track totes are a form of pool betting, the dividend paid to holders of winning bets being a share of the pool. Such dividends are the copyright of the tracks concerned (in greyhound racing each track operates its own tote) and bookmakers are not authorised to use them as a basis for settling bets.

A 'dual-forecast' is a variation of the forecast bet, offered by the Tote (*ie* Horserace Totalisator Board) at horse race meetings. It gives the cover of a 'reverse forecast' (*ie* it wins if the two nominated runners finish as the first two *in either order*) for *one* stake. This bet is also available to off-course bettors through the Tote's betting shop division, Tote Bookmakers, and certain other bookmakers licensed to bet at Tote odds.

Another form of forecast bet – available for greyhounds – is the 'dual-forecast treble'. This gives the cover of a 'reverse forecast' *for one unit stake*, enabling the bettor to cover, say, 3 greyhounds in each of 3 races for just 27 stakes instead of the 216 which would be required for straight forecast combinations. Some firms market this bet as a 'Triesta', in which case only specified advertised races are covered and special dividends and consolation dividends declared.

See Greyhound betting, Tote betting off-course, Tote Dual-forecast, Triesta

Form

'Form' is the performance history of a runner and the principal means of assessing its chance in a race. Evaluating form is essentially about ranking the runners in order of merit, according to their potential ability over the distance and, in the case of horses, with the weight carried.

Given the mass of information published in the press about a day's runners, 'studying form', at face value, has the appearance of an irksome and time-consuming business. Some people do, in fact, spend a lot of time delving in the form pages – not always, it has to be said, to good effect! Given the apparent magnitude of the task, it is not surprising that most bettors follow form at second-hand, by following the opinions of newspaper selectors, using published ratings or reacting to the sentiment of the market.

However, as observed elsewhere in this book, one of the drawbacks of following opinion-leaders (especially a successful one), as far as betting is concerned, is that because they *do* lead opinion, they may also have a downward effect on the odds – and *de facto* there is no value! Experts can save a great deal of duplication of effort and may give good advice, but they do not control the starting prices! So bettors, whatever help they receive from expert sources, must make themselves responsible for deciding if the odds are favourable.

There are two points about form that the bettor should always hold in mind. The first demonstrates that reading form may not be the awesome task it may at first appear. The other is a word of caution – which being largely unheeded by the betting public – can steer the bettor away from bad value towards good.

The first point. The press publishes a mass of information about the day's racing and runners, in great detail … but not all the information is meaningful. Much is merely 'noise' – background which gets in the way of the information which really counts. The press should not be blamed! The public has an insatiable appetite for more and more facts and newspapers merely provide what their readers want. The bettor must use intelligence to extract only what is useful.

The second point. 'Coincidence' is not form. You spin a coin four times. 'Heads' wins, then loses three times in a row. From that, it should not be concluded that 'heads' is not an 'even chance'! In other words, do not place reliance on one or two results if they do not fit the broader picture. The contender's overall standing is what counts. Horses, greyhounds and people have bad days or bad luck and therefore turn in the odd uncharacteristic results. But, in the end, it is class that counts.

The public, including many professionals, often over-reacts to a single poor result if it also happens to be the most recent one. That is why, on occasions, a class performer can notch a comfortable win at an amazingly good price!

See Selection methods, Value

Fractional odds

Odds are always stated in a manner whereby both sides are given as whole numbers. So, $1\frac{1}{2}/1$ (1.5/1) becomes 6/4, $2\frac{1}{2}/1$ (2.5/1) becomes 5/2, $2\frac{3}{4}/1$ (2.75/1) becomes 11/4 and so on. To convert fractional odds to odds-to-1, divide the lefthand figure by the righthand figure. A calculator gives the answer in decimal notation. Thus 15/8 is shown to be 1.875/1.

Bettors who have difficulty in grasping where fractional odds are located, see the table of odds on p. 70.

See Odds

Frame

Racecourse device for displaying the numbers of the first 4 horses to finish. Hence, the colloquial expression 'in the frame' means 'placed' – but usually in the more restricted sense of those runners which qualify for a payout.

Fringe betting

A term used to cover betting on contingencies, usually of a non-sporting kind, beyond the mainstream of events on which bookmakers routinely lay odds. The boundaries of fringe betting are necessarily vague. In 1959, betting on the outcome of a General Election might have been considered a fringe bet. Today, election betting can be big business, capable of generating more turnover than a major horse race such as the Derby. Thus, today's fringe bet may become a mainstream bet of the future.

Some firms positively relish the opportunity to enter into unusual bets, with the proviso that the bet be in good taste, from odds about the existence of yetis or of the Loch Ness Monster to quite serious propositions such as betting on future meteorological conditions.

It is also possible to obtain odds about contingencies in the future course of one's own life – such as the likelihood of having a multiple birth or of achieving a given personal ambition. Interested readers should consult the article by Graham Sharpe, an authority on the subject of fringe bets, in the 1991 edition of 'The Sporting Life Guide to How to Pick Winners' (see p. 127).

Full-cover

Term denoting every arrangement of forecasts or tricasts, or of doubles, trebles and accumulators, from a given number of selections.

For the number of bets needed for full-cover of different numbers of selections in forecasts and tricasts, see the tables on pages 42 and 118.

For the number of bets required for full-cover of different numbers of selections in multiple bets, see the table on page 66.

See All-ways, Limited cover, Multiple bets, Permutation

Gamble (n)

Although, strictly, the noun 'gamble' signifies any gambling transaction, in betting circles the word is usually taken to signify a flood of bets for a runner, often an outsider, forcing bookmakers to make drastic cuts in its odds.

How about a winner of your own to pick?

Why not become a Greyhound Owner?

For the best advice go to the top-phone the Racing Manager of your nearest GRA Stadium and seek his guidance. How to buy, the price to pay, finding a trainer – all you want to know. He'll tell you too about the £1½ million plus to be paid out in prize money at GRA race tracks in 1992, about the unique benefits GRA owners* receive and about the thrills and fun you – and all your family – can enjoy all year round.

*Including FREE admission to any GRA Stadium with the prized GRA Owner's Pass.

CATFORD STADIUM
Adenmore Rd. Catford Bridge
London SE6 4RJ
Tel: 081-690 2261

WIMBLEDON STADIUM
Plough Lane
London SW17 0BL
Tel: 081-946 5361

HALL GREEN STADIUM
York Road, Hall Green
Birmingham B28 8LQ
Tel: 021-777 1181

WEMBLEY STADIUM
Wembley HA9 0DW
Tel: 081-902 8833

BELLE VUE STADIUM
Kirkmanshulme Lane
Gorton
Manchester M18 7BA
Tel: 061-223 1266

PORTSMOUTH STADIUM
Target Road, Tipnor
Portsmouth PO2 8QU
Tel: 0705 663231

'Going in'

Betting shop announcement, warning that the greyhounds are entering the traps for the next race and that only a few moments remain for betting.

Goliath

Multiple bet covering 8 selections, in different events. Consists of 28 doubles, 56 trebles, 70 fourfolds, 56 fivefolds, 28 sixfolds, 8 sevenfolds and 1 eightfold. In all, 247 bets.
See Multiple bets

Goliath staking ready reckoner 8 selections 247 wagers 28 doubles/56 trebles/70 fourfolds/56 fivefolds/28 sixfolds/ 8 sevenfolds/1 eightfold					
Stake	Win	Each-way	Stake	Win	Each-way
0.05	12.35	24.70	0.30	74.10	148.20
0.10	24.70	49.40	0.35	86.45	172.90
0.15	37.05	74.10	0.40	98.80	197.60
0.20	49.40	98.80	0.45	111.15	222.30
0.25	61.75	123.50	0.50	123.50	247.00

Green Seal Service

Betting arbitration service provided by *The Sporting Life*, renowned for its impartial and authoritative opinions on betting matters. Many thousands of disputes are resolved, with its help, every year. Letters for Green Seal Service to: Green Seal Service, The Sporting Life, Orbit House, 1 New Fetter Lane, London EC4A 1AR. Please enclose an SAE.
See Disputes

Greyhound betting

Greyhound racing is second only in popularity to horse racing as a medium for betting, and is generally believed to account for about a quarter of off-course betting turnover. There is normally at least one, often two and sometimes three meetings on the daytime betting shop service. Such meetings are supplied by track promoters under contract to the Bookmakers' Afternoon

Greyhound Services Ltd (BAGS) as a service for betting shops. Nevertheless, they are in every sense normal meetings, attended by the public, and staged under the control of the track managements to the same high standard (as laid down by National Greyhound Racing Club rules) as every other greyhound meeting. Uniquely, all meetings from Hackney are on the daytime BAGS service, which means that bettors have the opportunity of following all the racing from that track, wherever they may live.

Greyhound bets available in betting shops are 'win', 'each-way', 'forecast' (1–2) and, in races of 6 runners or more, 'tricast' (1–2–3). Some shops offer dual-forecast (1–2 in either order) trebles (sometimes marketed for selected races only as a 'Triesta'), and a greyhound 'placepot' (a place-only starting price accumulator on 6 consecutive races).

The forecast 'dividend' paid to betting shop customers should not be confused with the dividend paid to racegoers at the track by the racecourse tote. Off-course forecasts on races on the daytime service are settled according to the 'BAGS computer forecast', which uses a formula based on the starting prices in the race in question. Similarly, there is a 'BAGS computer tricast' dividend. These dividends are announced shortly after each race and are reported in the press. A deduction for 'tax' is incorporated in the dividend calculations, so bettors should not add any 'tax' when making a forecast or tricast bet. Likewise, the dividends are paid in full. Dividends are declared to a £1 unit, so a 50p forecast would pay one-half the declared dividend.

Bets on major evening greyhound meetings may be made off-course at betting shops. Such bets are settled at official starting prices. Forecast bets on evening races are settled according to the 'Chart', literally a chart of dividends for the possible combinations of starting prices for the first and second greyhounds. Like the computer forecast, the Chart includes a provision for 'tax'.

Bets at some tracks, mainly smaller ones where the betting market is considered too weak to guarantee the return of reliably representative odds, may not be accepted. Up-to-date details of acceptable tracks, and the special payout limits which may be applied (which vary from bookmaker to bookmaker), should be checked against the firm's rules.

Greyhound racing is a very exciting 'live' spectacle. On-course betting is free of Betting Duty (although at some tracks there is a controversial 1% deduction from bookmakers' returns, which is paid to the track management for the 'improvement of racing and amenities').

As at horse race meetings, racegoers can choose between betting with a bookmaker or the tote (the latter being operated by the track management). The maximum retention from greyhound totes permitted by law was raised in December 1991 from $17\frac{1}{2}$% to 29%. That does not mean tracks will automatically increase their take-out to the maximum allowed. It would not be in their interest to do so (see 'Utility', p. 122). However, racegoers may wish to inform themselves about the stoppages on the various pools.

Track bookmakers only offer straight win bets. The tote offers a variety of bets. Most leading tracks have win, place, forecast, and trio (the name used at tracks for a 1–2–3 bet) pools, the last two being extremely popular with racegoers. Some tracks also have a special carry-forward pool which gives the racegoer the opportunity of winning a dividend of several thousand pounds for a very small stake.

The outcome of greyhound races is determined, like other sporting contests, by a blend of the known and the unknown. Because all the action of a greyhound race is compressed into a very small space of time (most races take about 30 seconds to run), the effect of random incidents tends to be more palpable to the spectator than they are in sporting events which unfold more slowly. An incident of bumping at the first bend which effectively wrecks the chance of a bettor's selection may be immensely disappointing, but such uncertainties should be accepted as part of the sport and a warning to bettors not to be too ready to wager on favourites at very short prices (in graded races at, say, odds of 5/4 and less).

As with other forms of betting, success depends on finding 'value', wagers offered at prices which underestimate a runner's ability in relation to the rest of the field. As a rule-of-thumb for 6-runner races, bettors should look for minimum odds for their selection of 2/1 on-course or 5/2 off-course in races where the selection appears to have *one* serious rival, and 3/1 on-course and 7/2 off-course where the selection appears to have *two* serious rivals. Apparent one-dog races should be regarded with caution. The cramped odds on offer usually make such stand-outs dubious betting propositions.

Greyhound races follow each other with great rapidity. The repetitive stream of races and the coincidences it throws up tend to encourage number betting and other forms of superstitious wagering. However, the bettor who is looking for a better-than-average return from his greyhound betting should disavow all such tendencies and be guided strictly by form.

'The Sporting Life Guide to Greyhound Racing & Betting'* is essential reading for anyone who wants to obtain an overall understanding of the sport and how to bet on it. There is also an informative article on the betting aspects of greyhound racing ('Greyhound value – at the track and in the betting shop' by David Bennett) in 'The Sporting Life Guide to How to Pick Winners' (see p. 127).

See BAGS, National Greyhound Racing Club, Open race, Placepot (greyhound), Re-runs, Reserves, Tricast, Triesta

Handicap

In horse racing, a race in which different weights are allotted to the runners by the official handicapper in order to 'equalise' their chances.

In greyhound racing, it is a race with a staggered (as opposed to level) start.

Handicapping makes possible the framing of races in which winners of mixed abilities can compete. Although, in theory, the handicapper is supposed to 'equalise' the chances of the runners, this is an unattainable ideal in practice which would presuppose that the handicapper had knowledge which was beyond human ken. However, the purpose of the handicapper is fulfilled so long as the penalties awarded muddy the available information about the abilities of the runners sufficiently to increase uncertainty and divide opinion.

See Chance

Handicap betting

Many American football and Rugby League or Rugby Union matches are unequal contests which, if priced up for betting, would necessarily mean a favourite at an unappealingly short price coupled with an outsider of little or no interest to bettors. Such matches can be turned into more interesting betting propositions by handicapping the favoured team by 'giving' the opposing side a number of points' start.

Let us take a Rugby League match between underdog Salford (+12) versus favourite Widnes. The result is 10–18, so Widnes win 'straight-up'. But, for betting purposes, Salford with 12 points to add to their score of 10 (giving a total of 22) are the winners on handicap.

---

*The first edition, published in 1988, is out-of-print. A new, revised, edition is due to be published during 1992

In setting the number of points of handicap, the aim of the oddsmaker is to divide betting opinion more or less equally, so that each team can be offered at the same (or similar) price. In Rugby League that price may be 4/5 or 5/6, with draw odds varying from 12/1 to 16/1. In American football, the odds are usually 10/11 'pick' (with no draws). In the United States, fluctuations in the demand for bets for one team or the other are accommodated by making changes in the 'pointspread', thereby attracting money in the desired direction. Many British bookmakers prefer to keep the handicap constant and influence the demand for bets by altering the odds about the two teams – offering, say, 4/5 for the preferred team and 1/1 the other, instead of 10/11 each.

For American football betting in Britain, points' start is usually given in half-points, thus eliminating drawn results. This practice avoids a 'push' – the American custom of returning stakes to bettors in the case of drawn results.

Bettors are sometimes confused by the mixture, in lists of matches, of plus (+) and minus (−) signs. Much of the confusion is due to the lack of a standardised practice used for displaying handicap terms. One way, unfavoured in British betting lists, puts the favourite's name on the left and the underdog's on the right, followed by the number of points to be added to the underdog's score. The home team is written in capitals. This has the advantage of expressing all the handicaps in one column in the same (+) terms. Thus:

Houston Oilers   NEW YORK JETS   +4½

However, the customary ways put the home team on the left:

New York Jets (+4½)   Houston Oilers

or (more confusingly) on the right:

Houston Oilers at New York Jets   −4½

(In this last case, the pointspread is expressed in terms of the 'away' team which, in this case, is the favourite, so the sign is a minus.)

A minus sign (−) indicates points *given*, while a plus sign (+) indicates points *received*. So the sign to be used depends on which team the bettor wants to back. The bettor who wants to wager on the Oilers (giving 4½) should write: 'Houston Oilers −4½'. The bettor who wants to wager on the Jets (receiving 4½) should write: 'New York Jets +4½'. The counter clerk should be asked to validate the handicap, and note and initial the price on the betting slip, as for any non-SP bet.

See American football, Spread, Straight-up

51

'Hare is running'

Betting shop announcement immediately prior to the start of a greyhound race and cue for betting shop staff to process the off-slip for that race. Any bets on the race taken in error after that point are void.

Hedging

To 'hedge' means to bet on an opposing result, to secure against loss – or to guarantee a win.

For example, the holder of a bet on a horse involved in a photo-finish may, if he is at the racecourse and the bookmakers are laying odds on the result of the photo, hedge with a 'saver' bet on the other runner in contention. This is opportunistic hedging.

Bookmakers themselves, especially of the racecourse kind, are very partial to opportunistic hedging.

However, it is in the field of ante-post betting (sports as well as racing) that hedging, as a serious art form, comes into its own. The idea is, as soon as the betting opens, to pick a contender (or contenders) at long odds, whose chance seems very much to have been underestimated by the odds-compiler. One need not necess-arily see the 'runner' as the ultimate winner. Merely as one with a very good chance of surviving to the closing stages of the competi-tion, by which time its odds will have been very much reduced.

Hedging takes place as soon as it is possible to bet on all the other survivors and be assured of a profit whichever wins.

Whether this method of wagering makes strict sense from a rational betting point of view is open to question, since it violates the general principle that betting decisions be left to the latest moment in order to bet with the benefit of any late-emerging information. But it is a form of wagering which offers sustained interest over a period of time and, since an important utility of betting for most bettors, is the fun provided, it has much to commend it as an economical form of entertainment!

The most able to take advantage of ante-post odds are those who obtain information before it breaks generally – always supposing they are able to penetrate the bookmaking industry's early-warning radars whose effectiveness is renowned!

Heinz

Multiple bet covering 6 selections in different events. Consists of 15 doubles, 20 trebles, 15 fourfolds, 6 fivefolds and 1 sixfold. In all, 57 bets.

See Multiple bets

	Heinz				
	staking ready reckoner				
	6 selections 57 wagers				
	15 doubles/20 trebles/15 fourfolds/6 fivefolds/1 sixfold				
Stake	Win	Each-way	Stake	Win	Each-way
0.05	2.85	5.70	0.55	31.35	62.70
0.10	5.70	11.40	0.60	34.20	68.40
0.15	8.55	17.10	0.65	37.05	74.10
0.20	11.40	22.80	0.70	39.90	79.80
0.25	14.25	28.50	0.75	42.75	85.50
0.30	17.10	34.20	0.80	45.60	91.20
0.35	19.95	39.90	0.85	48.45	96.90
0.40	22.80	45.60	0.90	51.30	102.60
0.45	25.65	51.30	0.95	54.15	108.30
0.50	28.50	57.00	1.00	57.00	114.00

Home bookmaker

Racecourse bookmaker betting on the racing at the meeting he is attending.

See Away bookmaker

Horse race betting

Horse racing is by far the most popular medium for betting. Of a total off-course betting turnover in 1990–91 in excess of £6,000m, 72% was wagered on horses (as compared to about 28% on greyhounds and other sports).

As revealed by a Levy Board survey (1989–90), bettors show distinct preferences with regard to the kind of race on which they like to bet:

● Flat racing is preferred to National Hunt. The turnover split between the two codes is 60:40.

● In Flat racing, the best quality racing (Group One, especially Classics) produces the biggest turnover, followed by handicaps. Selling, amateur and apprentice races are least popular.

● In National Hunt, there is a similar preference for quality, races such as the Grand National, Cheltenham Gold Cup and Champion Hurdle generating most betting interest. Selling races, hunter chases and NH flat races generate least interest.

● All-weather racing attracts less interest than turf.

● Bettors are less interested in races of fewer than 8 runners (although NH flat races are of little interest in spite of large fields).

In the period 1986–90, 36.2% of all Flat races were won by favourites (non-handicaps 42.2%, handicaps 29.1%). In the period 1986–91, 39.5% of all National Hunt races were won by favourites.

The over-round to which bookmakers bet varies from race to race, depending mainly on the number of runners. The over-round can be worked out exactly using the table given on p. 70 but, as a very rough rule-of-thumb, the bettor can expect 2 points of over-round for each runner in the field. The fixed win pool retention of 16% clearly makes the Tote probable good value in fields of, say, 10 runners or more.

See Racecourse betting

Horserace Betting Levy Board

The statutory body which negotiates the horse race betting levy with the bookmaking industry and administers the fund for the benefit of racing, breeding and veterinary science and education.

Address: Horserace Betting Levy Board, 52 Grosvenor Gardens. London SW1W 0AU. Telephone: 071-730 4540.

Horserace Totalisator Board

A public body instituted in 1928 to generate money to support horse racing through the operation of racecourse pool betting.

The present-day Tote also operates a betting shop subsidiary, Tote Bookmakers Ltd, which offers betting at Tote odds and normal starting price business. Another subsidiary, Tote Credit Ltd, offers a Tote and SP service for credit account customers both on and off the course.

Address: Horserace Totalisator Board, Tote House, 74 Upper Richmond Road, London SW15 2SU. Telephone: 081-874 6411.

See Tote

If-cash

Instruction to bookmaker to use a stated part of a return from prior bets to stake another selection, the 'if-cash' bet being conditional upon cash being in hand.

The 'if-cash' wager is technically a separate bet. Even if tax was prepaid on the original bet(s), tax is due on the return arising from the separate 'if-cash' element.

See Any-to-come

If-lose

Conditional wager indicating that a bet is required only if the antecedent selection loses. The term is understood by bookmakers to mean 'if lose or non-runner'.

If-win

Conditional wager indicating that a bet is required only if the antecedent selection wins. The term is understood by bookmakers to mean 'if win or non-runner'.

Immediate payout

Some betting shop companies offer immediate payout, at the manager's discretion, up to a stated amount, before the official weighed-in signal is given – retainable even if the placings are later changed as a result of an enquiry or objection.

Without such a dispensation, a bettor would not be justified in retaining 'winnings' paid in error reclaimed by the bookmaker.

Incorrect instructions

Incorrect instructions come in many forms and the problems caused are dealt with according to individual bookmakers' rules. Here are some examples and the usual way the difficulty is dealt with.

Too few bets

Where too few bets are instructed to cover the number of written selections, the total stake is usually divided and invested in proportion among the correct number of bets required.

Too few selections

Where there are too few selections for the stated number of bets, there are widely differing practices. Some firms, where a named multiple bet is involved, settle the whole stake in proportion for the correct number of doubles, trebles etc for the number of selections. Others invest for the correct bets to the stated unit and return the excess after all the selections have run. The *Sporting Life* view is that the error is best resolved by adding a non-runner or non runners so that the wager corresponds to the total stake invested. However, the bettor is bound by the bookmaker's rule – whatever it may be.

See Overstaking, Understaking

Incomplete or ambiguous instructions

Bookmakers' rules try to provide for every possibility, so the bettor who fails to give full or clear instructions will usually find there is still a provision for investing the stake – in one way or another! If that way is not what the bettor actually meant, he has only himself to blame!

What, for example, is a settler to make of a bet for Indian Monarch in a race in which no such runner takes part but in which there is an Indian Queen and a Dancing Monarch? Such ambiguities are normally resolved by equally dividing the stake and investing an equal part on each of the possible runners.

What should be done when no time or meeting is stated and the name of the selection could refer either to a horse or a greyhound running on the same day? Normally, the bet goes on the horse race, although if one has already run at the time the bet is placed, it stands for the one yet to run.

These and many other errors are covered by specific rules. But, needless to say, disappointment and bad feeling are best avoided by writing the slip fully and correctly in the first place, taking care, in particular, to: state meetings and times, spell the names of selections correctly, indicate the unit stake, state whether win or each-way is required, and stake the correct total.

See Unnamed selections

Inside

Term used by racecourse and greyhound track bookmakers to signify the main enclosure – as in the following, 'They're laying 6/4 inside' meaning 'The bookmakers of the main enclosure are laying 6/4'.

See Outside

Jackpot

See Tote Jackpot

Jockey Club

Governing body of horse racing in mainland Britain, with responsibility for the administration, organisation and control of both Flat and National Hunt (jumps) racing. It was founded about 1750.

As part of the general re-appraisal of how racing is organised in Britain, the Jockey Club has proposed a unifying body for the sport – a British Horseracing Board – in which the Jockey Club, owners, racecourses and the Horseracing Advisory Council would all play a part.

The Jockey Club appoints stewards to supervise race meetings to ensure that the racing is conducted in accordance with the rules.

Address: The Jockey Club, 42 Portman Square, London W1H 0EN. Telephone: 071-486 4921.

Jockeys' championship

Bets on the jockeys' championship, Flat or National Hunt, are settled on winning rides in the UK. Rides in other countries do not count.

Jockey's mount

Selection specified by name of rider. Problems can arise when the jockey in question rides fewer or more than the number of bets staked. Where there are fewer mounts than bets, the missing mounts are usually treated as non-runners. If the jockey rides more, then the number of singles, doubles and accumulators are determined by the actual number of mounts, the stake being divided and invested accordingly.

Joint

Equipment erected by racecourse bookmaker on his pitch from which to ply his trade. It consists principally of a board on which, race by race, is affixed the list of runners, against which the going prices are written. The other important article of bookmaker equipment is the sturdy satchel, suspended at the front of the joint, which acts as a receptacle for banknotes.

See Pitch

Kelly system

Term sometimes used for a staking method otherwise known as 'fixed fraction betting', so named after J. L. Kelly, a mathematician who studied it.

See Fixed fraction betting

Late withdrawal

In horse races (excluding ante-post bets) where a runner is withdrawn without coming under starter's orders or declared 'not to have started', the horse is treated as a non-runner (see 'Not under orders', p. 68). If there is insufficient time for a new betting market to be formed, winnings (exclusive of stake) are subject to a deduction laid down by 'Tattersalls Rules'. The amount of deduction depends on the prevailing odds of the withdrawn horse.

This rule and the reason for it are often not understood, so that disappointed customers believe they have been unfairly penalised.

The explanation is not so complicated. A bookmaker's margin of profit depends on laying all the runners in a field. The odds are shared out among them. If one of the runners is taken away, the bookmaker can no longer 'afford' the odds offered on the remaining runners. The Tattersalls scale of deductions is compensation for what are otherwise over-generous prices.

In greyhound racing, where there are withdrawals from a 'no-race' re-run later, backers of withdrawn greyhounds are on non-runners. 'Show' or 'early' prices taken on the remaining runners are cancelled and all bets are settled at SP.

See Not under orders, Tattersalls Rule 4c

'Law of averages'

Many bettors believe that nature incorporates a mechanism whereby winners are stored up in the future to compensate for losers in the past. They call it the 'law of averages' or the 'law of maturity of chances'.

Let us suppose a series of 100 coin-spins, of which the first 50 spins result in 30 'heads' and 20 'tails'. A believer in the so-called law of averages argues that, because the expected number of 'heads' in a series of 100 spins is about 50, only 20 'heads' to 30 'tails' are to be expected from the remaining 50 spins. To one who so reasons, 'tails' becomes a better bet from the fifty-first spin.

A follow-on from this line of thinking, is that, if a given number of 'losers' is counted-out without betting, followed by a resumption of betting, the bettor's chance of winning is enhanced.

Such notions are utterly fallacious. In the chosen example, the chance of 'heads' remains the same on each and every occasion – 50%, by virtue of the symmetry of the coin, regardless of what has gone before.

The law of averages is a misunderstanding of the 'Law of Large Numbers' which states that, as a series of trials (in the cited example, coin-spins) is extended towards infinity, so the *proportions* of the different outcomes ('heads' and 'tails') more closely approximate the probabilities (50%). However, this law does not predict numerical symmetry between the outcomes and, in fact, as the number of trials increases so does the numerical difference between the outcomes, although the divergence becomes less and less significant in proportion to the total number of trials.

Many roulette players are (fatally) addicted to the myths associated with the so-called law of averages.

Layer

Colloquial term for a bookmaker – one who 'lays', that is to say offers, odds.

Levy

Contribution to the racing industry raised primarily from off-course horse racing bets. The levy is paid for out of some of the difference between the actual rate of government Betting Duty and the 10% 'tax' on betting shop bets (see 'Tax', p. 109).

Levy Board

Short name for the Horserace Betting Levy Board.

See Horserace Betting Levy Board

Limited cover

Each increase in the number of selections in a multiple wager involves an escalating number of bets and corresponding number of stakes. A Heinz (6 selections), for example, comprises 57 bets, a Multi (7 selections) 120 bets, and a Goliath (8 selections) 247 bets – beyond the means of many bettors, even with a very small unit stake.

To cater for those who want to spread their bets over a number of selections and enjoy the possibility of a big win, while also limiting their total stake, betting shops offer a range of special multiple bets giving limited selective cover. A 'Union Jack', for example, consists of 8 trebles from 9 selections, where full-cover would require 84 trebles!

Most selective cover multiple bets are marketed under the special product names of individual firms, who supply special printed slips carrying details of the bet and any bonuses offered.

Opting for limited cover necessarily surrenders much to the whims of fate! In a Union Jack, for example, it is possible to have 6 winning selections without a return.

See Full-cover, Multiple bets

Limits

Over the long term even the improbable can happen. So bookmakers, no matter how great their resources, have to protect themselves by setting 'limits' against the day when someone lands a spectacularly lucky accumulator of longshots capable of wiping them out!

Bookmakers' limits take two forms. On the one hand, there is an overall maximum payout to any one client in respect of a single day's betting which, in the case of a big firm, may be up to £500,000 – sufficient to make the average bettor comfortable for life! Drastically lower limits are set for bets on events after 6.30pm and other events not covered in full by the betting shop news service: evening horse racing, non-BAGS greyhound racing and foreign racing, for example. Such reduced limits govern accumulative bets that include winners at any such meeting.

Small bookmakers may also impose 'across-the-card' limits, which limit the payout where there are successful selections in 2 or more races run at or nearly the same time.

Because of their limited resources, small bookmakers' limits are dwarfed by those offered by the large chains. Bettors using multiple bets capable of landing huge odds owe it to themselves to check their bookmaker's rules, before their lucky day arrives, to ensure the limits are sufficient to cover a big payout in full.

The other way in which a betting shop (or course bookmaker) can limit liability is to refuse to accept a bet, or to accept it only at a reduced stake or reduced odds, or a combination of both.

For example, a bettor wishing to place an ante-post £400 each-way bet at odds of 50/1 may be 'cut back' to £200 each-way at 50/1 and the rest at 25/1. This line of defence, sometimes deemed necessary by the bookmaker to balance ante-post commitments on an event, is a common cause of misunderstanding between bookmaker and client.

Ultimately, limits are a protection for the public as well as the bookmaker. The notorious moonlight disappearances of betting shops in the mid-19th century – which led to the outlawing of off-course cash betting for over 100 years – was mainly due to the lack of rules on limits and of proper control of liabilities, and the inability, therefore, of the promoters to ride out a bad result.

Line

American term for the advertised odds or pointspread for a coming event.

Longshot

A runner at 'long' odds with little chance.
See Outsider

Losing streaks

'Losing streaks' are uninterrupted series of losers. Needless to say, every bettor dreads them, in particular the long ones which become a depressing drain on resources. Unfortunately, everyone who dabbles with chance has to experience them.

Of course, there are 'winning streaks', too. But because the bettor is usually betting 'odds-against', they are shorter on average and come less often.

The average length of losing streaks depends upon the bettor's long-term strike-rate (*ie* winners to bets). Someone succeeding 12 times in every 100 bets, on average, will necessarily fare worse than someone achieving 33 per 100, although even the latter will experience some very disheartening series (see sample results on facing page).

Among the chestnuts that are passed off as betting wisdom are several superstitions involving losing and winning runs. One of the

```
L W L W W L W L W L L W W L W W L L L L L L W W L W L W L L L W W L L W W W W L L L L L W L L L L L
L W L W L L L W L L W L L W W L L L L W W W L L W L W L W L L L W L L L L L L L W L L L L W L L W
L W L W W L W W L W L W L L L W W L L L L L L W L L L L L L L W L L W L L L L L L L L L W L L L L L L
W W L W W W L W L W L L L L L L L W L W L W L L L L L W L L L W L L W W L W W L W W W L L L L L L W L
L W L L W L W L W L W L L L W W L L W L L L L L L L L L L L L L L L W L L W W L L L L W W W L L L L L W
L L L L L W L L L W L L L W L L L L L L L W W L L W L W L L L W L W L L L L L L L W L W L L L L L L L W L
W W L L L W L L L L L L L W L L L L L L W L L W L L W L L L W L W L L L L L L W L W L L L L L L L L L L
W L W W W L L L L L L W L W W W W L L L L L L L L L L L L W L W L L L L W L L W L L W L L W L L L L L L L L
L W W W L L L L L L L L L L W L L W L L L L L L W L W L L W W L L L L L L L L W W L L L L L L L W L W L L
W W L L L L L W L L W W W W L W W W W L W W L L L W W W W L L W L L L L W L L L W W W L L L L L L L W W W
L W W W W L L L L L L L L W L W W L L L L L L L L W W W L L L L L W W L L L W L L W L L W L L W L L W L L
L L W L L L W W W W W L W L W L L W L W L L L W L W L W L W L W L W W W L L L W L W L L W L L W L L
L L W L W W W W W L L L L W L L L L L L L L L L L L L L W W L L W W L L L L L L L L W L W L W L W L L W
W W L L L L L W W L L W L L W W L L W L L W L W L W W W W L W W W L L L L L L L L L L L W L L L L W L L L L
W W L L W W L L L L L L W L L L W L W L L W W L L L L W L W L L W L L W L W L L L L L L L L L W L L W L L
L W L L L L L L L W L L L W L L L L W L L L W L L W L L W L L W L L W W L L W L L L L L L L L L L L L L L
W W L W L L L L L W L L L L W L L L W L W W L L L W L L W L L W L W L W L W L L L W W L L L L L L L L L L L
L L L W L L L L L W L L L L L W L L L W W L L L L L W L L L W L W L L L W L L L L L W L L L W L L W W L L W
```

```
L L L L L L L W L W L L L L L L L L L L L L W L L L L L L L L L L W L L L L L L L L W L L L W L L L L L W
L L L W L W L L L L L L L L L L L L L L L L L L L L L L L L L L L L L L L L L W L W L W L W L L L L L L L
L L L L L L L L L L L L L L L L L L L W L L L L L L W L L W L L L W L L L L L L L L L L L L L L L L L L L
W L L L L L L L L L L L L L L L L L L L W L W L L L W W L L W L L L L L W L L L L L L L L L L L L L L L L L
L L L W L L L W L L L L L L L L L L L L L L L L L W L W L L L L W L L L L L L L L L L L L L L W L L L L L L
L W W L L L L L L W L L W L L W L L L L L L L L L L L W L L L L W L W L W L W L L W L L L L L L L L L L L W W
L L W L L L L W W L L L L L L L L L L L L L L L L L L W L L L L L W L L L L L L L L L L L L W L L L L L L
L L L W L L L L L W L L L L L L L L L L L L L L L L L L L L L W W L L W L L L L W L L W L L L L L L L W L L L
L L L L L W L L L L L L L L L L L W L L W L L L L L L W L L L L L L L L W L L L L W L L L W L L L L L L L W L
L L L L L W L L L L L L L L L L L L L L W L L L L L L L L L L L W L W L L L L L W W L L L L W W L L L L L L
L L L L L L L L L L W L L L W L L L W L L L L L L L L L L L L L W L W L L L L L W W L L L L L W W L L L L L
W L L L L L W L L L L L L L L L L L L L L L L L L L L L L W L L L W W L L L L W L W L L L L L L L L L L W L L
L W L L L L L L L L L L L W L L W L L L L L L L L L L L L L L L L L L W L L L L L L L W L L L L L L L L L L
L L L L L W L L L L W W L L L L L L L L L L L L L L L L L W L W L L L L L L L L L L L L W L W L W L L L L L W
L L L L L L L L L L L L L L L L L W L L L L L L L L W L L L L L L L L L L L L L L L W L L L L L L L L
L L L L L W W L W L W L L L L L L L L L L L W L L L L L L L L L W L L L L L L L L L L L L L L L L L L L L
L L L W L L L L L L L L L W L L L L L L L L L L L L L L L W L L L L L L L L L L L W L L L L L L L L
L L L L L L L W L L L L L L L L L L L L L L L L L L L L L L W L L L L L L L L L L L L L L L L L W L
W L L L L L L W L L L L L L L L L L L L L L L W L L L L L L L L L L L L L L L L L L L L L L L L L L L L
```

Sample results for bets of different probabilities

most persistent is the idea that a winning bet is more likely after a run of losers than at another time. Another holds that, when a bettor is experiencing a run of winners, he is 'hot' and should capitalise by increasing stakes. Both ideas (which are contradictions) are fallacies.

No significance should be attached to the order in which winners and losers occur. Losing and winning streaks do not follow a pattern. Any apparent pattern is entirely coincidental. The length of a losing (or winning) streak has no bearing on the result of the next bet. The bettor should base his betting strategy solely on the merits of each proposed bet without being influenced by any series of antecedent winning or losing bets.

The long-term *ratio* of winners to losers is determined by the general policy on which the bettor makes his selections. The *order* in which good and bad results occur is determined by chance and is entirely random.

Luck

'Luck' is a concept much referred to in betting, often in a superstitious way. Luck is merely that property of nature whereby favourable (or unfavourable) events occur in an entirely unpredictable
way. However, belief in lucky numbers, lucky seats, lucky days,
lucky names, lucky tote windows and the like contradict that
principle, since they are founded on the belief that nature is *not*
arbitrary but inclined to act favourably (or unfavourably) toward an
individual when (or unless) suitably propitiated.

Superstitious bettors are not, of their nature, prone to rational
reflection. Otherwise they might ask 'What is nature to do, given
Bettor A whose lucky colour is Red, and Bettor B, whose lucky
colour is Yellow? Should the jockey in the Red silks or in the Yellow
silks be allowed to win?'!

In truth, nature is ruthlessly indifferent. However, luck does offer
its devotees one guarantee. While, on the one hand, their betting
will never, in the long term, rise above the average rate of loss
(whatever it happens to be for a given betting situation), likewise
the same bettor will not fall, in the long term, into a greater-than-
average rate of loss. As there is no rational relationship between
betting decisions founded on luck alone and the outcome of races,
the superstitious bettor's successes and failures are entirely random.
Such a bettor automatically becomes the captive of averageness.

Lucky 15

Multiple bet consisting of 15 wagers from 4 selections: 4 singles, 6
doubles, 4 trebles, and a fourfold accumulator (*ie* a Yankee plus
singles).

Betting shops usually supply special printed slips for this bet –
often carrying details of bonuses and/or consolations.
See Lucky 31, Lucky 63, Patent

Lucky 31

Multiple bet consisting of 31 wagers from 5 selections: 5 singles, 10
doubles, 10 trebles, 5 fourfolds, and a fivefold (*ie* a Super Yankee
plus singles).

Betting shops usually supply special printed slips for this bet –
often carrying details of bonuses and/or consolations on offer.
See Lucky 15, Lucky 63, Patent

Lucky 63

Multiple bet consisting of 63 wagers from 6 selections: 6 singles, 15
doubles, 20 trebles, 15 fourfolds, 6 fivefolds and a sixfold (*ie* a

Lucky 15
staking ready reckoner
4 selections 15 wagers
4 singles/6 doubles/4 trebles/1 fourfold

Stake	Win	Each-way	Stake	Win	Each-way
0.05	0.75	1.50	0.55	8.25	16.50
0.10	1.50	3.00	0.60	9.00	18.00
0.15	2.25	4.50	0.65	9.75	19.50
0.20	3.00	6.00	0.70	10.50	21.00
0.25	3.75	7.50	0.75	11.25	22.50
0.30	4.50	9.00	0.80	12.00	24.00
0.35	5.25	10.50	0.85	12.75	25.50
0.40	6.00	12.00	0.90	13.50	27.00
0.45	6.75	13.50	0.95	14.25	28.50
0.50	7.50	15.00	1.00	15.00	30.00

Lucky 31
staking ready reckoner
5 selections 31 wagers
5 singles/10 doubles/10 trebles/5 fourfolds/1 fivefold

Stake	Win	Each-way	Stake	Win	Each-way
0.05	1.55	3.10	0.55	17.05	34.10
0.10	3.10	6.20	0.60	18.60	37.20
0.15	4.65	9.30	0.65	20.15	40.30
0.20	6.20	12.40	0.70	21.70	43.40
0.25	7.75	15.50	0.75	23.25	46.50
0.30	9.30	18.60	0.80	24.80	49.60
0.35	10.85	21.70	0.85	26.35	52.70
0.40	12.40	24.80	0.90	27.90	55.80
0.45	13.95	27.90	0.95	29.45	58.90
0.50	15.50	31.00	1.00	31.00	62.00

Heinz plus singles).
See Lucky 15, Lucky 31, Patent

Mug

Slang term used by card sharps and the like for any gullible person who can be persuaded to join a crooked card game or play the 'three-card trick'. In former times, such tricksters haunted race-courses and race trains. It was thus a small step for racecourse bookmakers (in the first place, perhaps, the dishonest ones on the fringes of the trade known as 'welshers' who bolted when they made a losing book) to begin using the term as a disdainful collo-quialism for the customers who, in their opinion, were foolish enough to provide them with a living.
See Face

Multi

Multiple bet (also known as a Super Heinz) covering 7 selections. Consists of 21 doubles, 35 trebles, 35 fourfolds, 21 fivefolds, 7 sixfolds, and 1 sevenfold. In all, 120 bets.
See Multiple bets

Lucky 63 staking ready reckoner 6 selections 63 wagers 6 singles/15 doubles/20 trebles/15 fourfolds/6 fivefolds/1 sixfold					
Stake	Win	Each-way	Stake	Win	Each-way
0.05	3.15	6.30	0.55	34.65	69.30
0.10	6.30	12.60	0.60	37.80	75.60
0.15	9.45	18.90	0.65	40.95	81.90
0.20	12.60	25.20	0.70	44.10	88.20
0.25	15.75	31.50	0.75	47.25	94.50
0.30	18.90	37.80	0.80	50.40	100.80
0.35	22.05	44.10	0.85	53.55	107.10
0.40	25.20	50.40	0.90	56.70	113.40
0.45	28.35	56.70	0.95	59.85	119.70
0.50	31.50	63.00	1.00	63.00	126.00

	Multi (Super Heinz)				
	staking ready reckoner				
	7 selections 120 wagers				
	21 doubles/35 trebles/35 fourfolds/21 fivefolds/7 sixfolds/1 sevenfold				
Stake	**Win**	**Each-way**	**Stake**	**Win**	**Each-way**
0.05	6.00	12.00	0.55	66.00	132.00
0.10	12.00	24.00	0.60	72.00	144.00
0.15	18.00	36.00	0.65	78.00	156.00
0.20	24.00	48.00	0.70	84.00	168.00
0.25	30.00	60.00	0.75	90.00	180.00
0.30	36.00	72.00	0.80	96.00	192.00
0.35	42.00	84.00	0.85	102.00	204.00
0.40	48.00	96.00	0.90	108.00	216.00
0.45	54.00	108.00	0.95	114.00	228.00
0.50	60.00	120.00	1.00	120.00	240.00

Multiple bets

The object of a multiple bet is to try to give the best of all worlds – a small return for a partly-successful bet and the possibility of a very big return if all the selections succeed.

Full-cover multiple bets combine a given number of selections in doubles, trebles and accumulators. For example, the Trixie (4 bets from 3 selections), the Yankee (11 bets from 4 selections), the Super Yankee (26 bets from 5 selections), and so on.

Some multiple bets also include 'singles' (the Patent, for example), assuring a return even if only one selection succeeds.

The more ambitious multiple wagers involve large numbers of bets and corresponding numbers of stakes. A Heinz (6 selections), for example, comprises 57 bets, a Multi (7 selections) 120 bets, and a Goliath (8 selections) 247 bets – beyond the means of many bettors, even with a very small unit stake.

To cater for those who want to spread their bets over several selections and enjoy the possibility of a big win, while also limiting their total stake, betting shops offer a range of special multiple bets giving limited selective cover. A 'Union Jack', for example, consists of 8 trebles from 9 selections, where full-cover would require 84!

Opting for limited cover necessarily surrenders much to the whims of fate! In a Union Jack, for example, it is possible to have 6 winning selections without a return. That risk is the price which has to be paid for selectivity.

Multiple bets, in general, are a very profitable area of business for the bookmaker. The accumulative elements automatically 'play up' winnings so that the bettor is, in effect, staking a great deal more than the modest initial stakes would suggest. A bettor would probably take a different view of money management if he were staking a successful accumulator on a bet-by-bet basis! However, the fact that multiple bets have much to offer in terms of fun and hope for a small affordable *initial* outlay cannot be denied – but, at least, the bettor should enter the world of multiple bets with open eyes and understand why the bookmakers love them!

Full-cover multiple bets

Number of selections	Total bets (name)	Doubles	Trebles	4-folds	5-folds	6-folds	7-folds	8-folds	9-folds	10-folds	11-folds	12-folds
2	1	1										
3	4 (Trixie)	3	1									
4	11 (Yankee)	6	4	1								
5	26 (Super Yankee)	10	10	5	1							
6	57 (Heinz)	15	20	15	6	1						
7	120 (Multi)	21	35	35	21	7	1					
8	247 (Goliath)	28	56	70	56	28	8	1				
9	502	36	84	126	126	84	36	9	1			
10	1013	45	120	210	252	210	120	45	10	1		
11	2036	55	165	330	462	462	330	165	55	11	1	
12	4083	66	220	495	792	924	792	495	220	66	12	1

Nap

Tipster's best selection of the day. The term is derived from 'Napoleon', a nickname for a French gold coin worth 20 francs.

NARBOL

NARBOL (National Association of Racecourse Betting Offices Ltd) is a bookmakers' organisation franchised by the Racecourse Association to operate betting shops at racecourses. NARBOL offers a service similar to an off-course betting shop, taking wagers at small stakes, accumulative and multiple bets and other wagers not available in the ring or from the Tote, as well as normal 'win' bets. NARBOL shops bet on racing at other meetings taking place on the day, including greyhounds. NARBOL does not lay board prices.

In common with other betting at racecourses, bets are not liable for Betting Duty. However, NARBOL deducts 6% from returns, of which 5% is paid to the racecourse towards improved facilities and 1% is retained by NARBOL as a contribution to administration costs.

Address: National Association of Racecourse Betting Offices Ltd, Fairfield, Manston Lane, Cross Gates, Leeds LS15 8AJ. Telephone: (0532) 640241.

See Racecourse betting

National Association of Bookmakers Ltd (NAB)

Trade association of bookmakers, in effect a national voice for 13 regional bookmakers' associations, such as the Bookmakers' Protection Association (Southern Area), the Bookmakers' Association of Wales, and so on. Each local association is responsible for the administration and allotment of bookmakers' pitches at the racecourses within its area on behalf of the racing authorities.

Address: National Association of Bookmakers Ltd, Tolworth Tower (4th floor), Ewell Road, Surbiton, Surrey KT6 7EL. Telephone: 081-390 8222.

National Greyhound Racing Club (NGRC)

The body whose rules govern the principal greyhound venues in mainland Britain. Betting shops do not normally bet on greyhound races at meetings not licensed by the NGRC.

The NGRC was set up in 1928 to regulate and police what was then a new sport. It was created along the lines of the Jockey Club, upon whose rules those of the NGRC were based.

Address: National Greyhound Racing Club Ltd, 24–28 Oval Road, London NW1 7DA. Telephone: 071-267 9256.

See Greyhound betting

National Sporting League (NSL)

Bookmakers' trade association, founded in 1902. Membership is open to approved bookmakers on- or off-course. In the main, the NSL represents smaller firms, in particular, the smaller 'independent' betting shop.

The NSL publishes the NSL Forecast Chart which is an accepted basis, where a 'computer dividend' is not declared, for settling off course forecast wagers on horses and greyhounds.

Address: National Sporting League, Francis House, Francis Street, London SW1P 1DE. Telephone: 071-630 0234.

See Chart

Non-runner

Strictly speaking, a non-runner means what it says – a horse or grey-hound on the card which does not, in fact, take part in the race.

If a withdrawal is made from a horse race after the racecourse betting market has been formed, special rules apply.

But the term 'non-runner' also crops up in other contexts in betting shop rules, usually as a device for resolving difficulties of interpreting betting slip instructions.

See Late withdrawal

Not under orders

In horse racing, a signal is given just before the start of a race to indicate that the runners are 'under starter's orders'. Any horse withdrawn before coming under starter's orders is a non-runner (see 'Late withdrawal', p. 57).

Under a new rule introduced in 1992, the starter – in National Hunt racing only – may deem that a horse has not started when the whole body of the horse has failed to cross the line within a reasonable time or has crossed the line without its rider. A bet on such a runner would be void and Rule 4 deductions would apply to other bets.

See Late withdrawal, Tattersalls Rule 4c

Novelty bets

As part of their overall bets packages for major sporting events such as the Grand National, Cup Final, Super Bowl and so on, book-makers usually include a novelty bet or two – designed to reach those parts of the public other bets cannot reach! Such bets include odds for 'Number of finishers' (Grand National), 'Highest break of championships' (World Snooker), 'Total number of points scored in each pool' (Rugby World Cup), and the like.

Press commentators often issue health-warnings to their readers to avoid such offers and to concentrate instead on the more straight-forward betting opportunities. In a general sense, they are right to do so, since bookmakers tend to set the over-round of novelty bets on the high side, which means less money returned to bettors in winnings.

On the other hand, whenever bookmakers enter relatively unexplored territory, they are always a little vulnerable – from the possibility of miscalculated odds or other oversight. A celebrated example of a novelty bet gone wrong for some bookmakers involved odds for a golf hole-in-one. It was reported in 1990 that a group of bettors in the Midlands obtained odds of 14/1 and more from various betting shops against this occurring in the course of a tournament. The 'true' odds are reckoned to be no more than 7/4!

Even if, overall, novelty bets are bad value, they are worth scrutinising for the occasional overlay.

Objection

In horse racing, complaint by a runner's connections about the conduct of a race, such as bumping, boring, crossing-over or other infringement of the rules by another runner. Bets are normally not paid out until the racecourse Stewards have declared whether the placings should stand or be altered. However, some betting shops offer 'first past the post' settlement as an option.

At the racecourse, betting sometimes takes place on the outcome of objections.

See First past the post, Racing rules

Odds

The 'odds', as laid by bookmakers, are a statement of the terms of a bet without reference to money. ('Probabilities' [see p. 82] may also be expressed in odds form, but bookmakers' odds – meaning the terms of a bet – and probabilities are different entities and should not be confused on account of the shared notation.)

There are two sides to bookmakers' odds: on the left, the stake put up by the bookmaker; on the right, the stake put up by the bettor. Thus, odds of 3/1 are a stake by the bookmaker of 3 units and a stake by the bettor of 1 unit. In the case of odds of 1/3, the bookmaker's stake is 1 unit and the bettor's stake is 3 units.

By convention, dictated by practical considerations, the bookmaker offers (or 'lays') the odds, while the bettor quantifies the unit of the bet (£1, £5, £100 or whatever he considers prudent under the circumstances). The bookmaker acts as the stakeholder, holding both stakes until the race is determined.

If a bet at 3/1 wins, the bookmaker pays the bettor 3 units and returns the bettor's stake which he has been holding in trust. If the bet loses, the bookmaker pays the bettor's stake to himself.

This explanation, for clarity, ignores the effect of 'tax' deductions which enters into off-course transactions.

Odds are always stated in a manner whereby both sides can be given in whole numbers. Thus, fractional odds such as $1\frac{1}{4}/1$, $1\frac{1}{2}/1$ and $1\frac{3}{4}/1$ become 5/4, 6/4 and 7/4 (see the list of odds on p. 70).

Odds which truly reflect chances are called 'fair'. However, since the bookmaking industry has to pay its expenses and make a profit, the odds available on the racecourse or in a betting shop are 'unfair' or, in bookmaking parlance, 'over-round', to allow an element of profit.

Odds, odds-to-1 and percentage conversion table

Odds	Odds-to-1	%	Odds	Odds-to-1	%
1/5	0.20	83.3	2/1	2.00	33.3
2/9	0.22	81.8	85/40	2.12	32.0
1/4	0.25	80.0	9/4	2.25	30.8
2/7	0.29	77.8	5/2	2.50	28.6
30/100	0.30	76.9	11/4	2.75	26.7
1/3	0.33	75.0	3/1	3.00	25.0
4/11	0.36	73.3	100/30	3.33	23.1
2/5	0.40	71.4	7/2	3.50	22.2
4/9	0.44	69.2	4/1	4.00	20.0
40/85	0.47	68.0	9/2	4.50	18.2
1/2	0.50	66.7	5/1	5.00	16.7
8/15	0.53	65.2	11/2	5.50	15.4
4/7	0.57	63.6	6/1	6.00	14.3
8/13	0.61	61.9	13/2	6.50	13.3
4/6	0.67	60.0	7/1	7.00	12.5
8/11	0.73	57.9	15/2	7.50	11.8
4/5	0.80	55.6	8/1	8.00	11.1
5/6	0.83	54.5	17/2	8.50	10.5
10/11	0.91	52.4	9/1	9.00	10.0
20/21	0.95	51.2	10/1	10.00	9.1
evens	1.00	50.0	11/1	11.00	8.3
21/20	1.05	48.8	12/1	12.00	7.7
11/10	1.10	47.6	14/1	14.00	6.7
6/5	1.20	45.5	16/1	16.00	5.9
5/4	1.25	44.4	18/1	18.00	5.3
11/8	1.38	42.1	20/1	20.00	4.8
6/4	1.50	40.0	25/1	25.00	3.8
13/8	1.62	38.1	33/1	33.00	2.9
7/4	1.75	36.4	40/1	40.00	2.4
15/8	1.88	34.8	50/1	50.00	2.0
			100/1	100.00	1.0

When bets are struck at fair odds, there is no gain, in the long term, to either party to the bet. For example, in a coin-spinning situation (where each face has an equal chance of appearing), betting on 'heads' at fair odds of 1/1 will not lead to a significant loss or gain, in the long term, to either bettor or layer. However, the same chance backed at 4/5 would result in a long term average loss to the bettor of £10 per £100 staked.

Laying unfair odds is the principle upon which commercial betting – casino games and slot machines as well as bookmaking – is based.

However, from an odds point of view, there is an important difference between gambling artefacts, such as dice and roulette wheels, and sporting events. In the former, the true odds can be known exactly. Payout-odds to assure a given level of profit for the promoter can therefore be accurately determined. The true odds for a contender in a sporting event, on the other hand, cannot be known with certainty – it is a matter of opinion, and like all opinions liable to vary from individual to individual.

At one time, it was believed that the business of professional odds-laying for sporting events such as horse racing depended upon astute estimation of chances based on superior knowledge of the sport or on inside information. Then, in the early 19th century, it was realised that, so long as the *overall* set of odds included a margin of profit and that *all* the runners could be laid in various proportions, it was not necessary to know the true chances of the individual runners at all. Immense fortunes accrued to the pioneers of modern bookmaking who put into effect the new-found principle.

To show how it works, let us imagine a hypothetical match between two horses, Alpha and Beta. No matter what their relative chances, a profit is assured to the odds-layer if he can find two people, one willing to back Alpha at 4/5 and another to back Beta at 4/5, for identical stakes, say £500 on each side. Whichever horse wins, the promoter of the bets collects £500 in stake money but only has to pay out £400 in winnings, a gain of £100 – irrespective of the victor and how the race is run.

Let us bring this example closer to the real world by imagining that, instead of one backer for each horse, there are 6 for Alpha and 4 for Beta, all wanting to stake £100 each. The bookmaker meets this contingency by laying differential odds – making Alpha 1/2, reflecting the greater demand, and Beta 5/4. If Alpha wins, the bookmaker pays out £300 in winnings and keeps £400 in stake money, pocketing £100 profit. If Beta wins, the bookmaker pays out

£500 in winnings and keeps £600 stake money, again a profit of £100.

Real betting situations are made vastly more complicated by larger fields, many more bettors, varying stakes and, in the case of racecourse betting, the small amount of time available for trading bets. Such constraints lead to all kinds of imperfections – some winners being more profitable than others, some races leaving the bookmaker out of pocket – but in the long term such imperfections even out.

So long as the *overall* set of odds contains a margin of profit and the bookmaker makes a reasonable stab at guessing the proportions in which the public will wish to bet on the different contenders, the bookmaker is assured of a long term gain irrespective of which runner wins and its true odds.

Opportunities for the bettor to make a gain from betting lie in the fact that the odds laid by the bookmaker for any one particular runner need not always be a reflection of its chance (or 'probability'). The main criterion which determines how the odds are shared out among the runners is the demand for bets. Whenever the 'crowd' and the form book part company, an opportunity for a 'value bet' may appear. A value bet is one in which the price on offer underestimates the runner's actual chance of winning.

To calculate the amount of potential profit in a set of bookmaker's odds, each odds in the set must be translated into its percentage equivalent. On such a scale, 0 equals 'no chance at all' and 100 equals 'certainty'. All the other chances lie between, including an 'even chance' which occupies the mid-point of 50 (see table on p. 70). A percentage from odds is found thus: $(100/(odds+1))$. Odds from a percentage: $((100/percentage)-1)$.

If the odds were fair, the total of the percentages would be 100 exactly. But, in practice, the total will be found to exceed 100. The excess is called 'over-round'. The greater the excess, the greater the margin of potential profit.

The following are the odds and equivalent percentage figures for a greyhound race at Hackney:

		%
Trap 1	2/1	33
Trap 2	6/1	14
Trap 3	5/1	17
Trap 4	6/1	14
Trap 5	6/1	14
Trap 6	3/1	25
Total		**117**

In this case, the over-round is 17, giving the bookmaker a potential profit of 14.5% on turnover (17/117ths), providing he is able to lay all the runners in proportion to the percentages.

Should the percentages sum to less than 100, the 'book' is 'under-round' and weighted in favour of the betting public. Occasionally, though infrequently, this actually occurs.

The bettor who makes a habit of checking over-round will soon discover how much it varies from event to event. The knowledge can be used to advantage. By limiting bets to those occasions where the over-round is less than average, the bettor, from this one factor alone, can expect to obtain a much better return from his betting.

Football and other sports betting odds advertised by bookmakers vary from firm to firm, so that the overall book, calculated on the basis of the best terms available for each possible result, is diminished, sometimes to the point of being under-round. It clearly pays the bettor to look for the firm offering the best terms for the outcome of his choice.

See Bookmaker, Probability, Tax, Value

Odds-against

Terms of a wager in which the bookmaker puts up a stake greater than the bettor. In the case of 'odds-against' of 2/1, for example, the bookmaker stakes 2 units to the bettor's 1 unit.

See Evens, Odds, Odds-on

Odds-on

Terms of a wager in which the bookmaker stakes less than the bettor. In the case of 'odds-on' of 1/2, for example, the bookmaker stakes 1 unit to the bettor's 2.

See Evens, Odds, Odds-against

Off-slip

Special slip, used as a security measure, which is passed through the till when an 'off' is announced. The serial number recorded on the off-slip can be used to determine whether a bet was placed before or after the 'off'. A bet with a serial number higher than the number on the off-slip for that race is void, win or lose, and the stake is returnable to the backer.

Open race

At a greyhound track, a type of race for dogs of superior ability, open to entries from all licensed trainers and licensed tracks. The big events of the greyhound calendar, such as the Derby (at

Wimbledon) and Grand National (at Hall Green, Birmingham) are examples of open races, but there are also many smaller events throughout the year. Many betting shops will take bets on any open race (regardless of other provisions about approved venues), provided racecard and result are published in *The Sporting Life*. However, check the rules before betting. The *Life*, in practice, covers all NGRC opens.

See Greyhound betting

'Orders'

Means 'Under starter's orders' – a betting shop announcement warning that the start of a horse race is imminent.

See Not under orders

Outside

Term used by racecourse or greyhound track bookmakers to signify enclosures other than the main enclosure.

See Inside

Outsider

Unfancied runner offered at long odds.

Although long odds are superficially attractive, horse racing and greyhound racing statistics show that the margin of profit to bookmakers is much greater on outsiders than runners at short odds. Generally speaking, the bettor cannot expect much value in this area and should limit selections in the main to shorter-priced runners.

Over-and-under bet

An American-style sports bet, in which the bettor wagers whether the combined final score of both teams is over or under a stipulated number set by the bookmaker. For example, the posted number for a match between the New Orleans Saints and Chicago Bears might be 43. If the final score is 27–21 an 'over' bet wins. If the combined score is 24–13 an 'under' bet wins. It does not matter which team prevails. The aim of the layer is to set a number which gets two-sided action, at, say, 5/6 either side. A combined score equalling the posted number is known as a 'push' resulting in stakes being returned to bettors. 'Pushes' would not be practicable, off-course, in Britain because of Betting Duty law.

Over-broke

A set of odds in which a backer can bet on all the runners and be sure of a profit is said to be 'over-broke'. Over-broke conditions,

while rare, can nevertheless occasionally arise in the hurly-burly of on-course betting.
See Odds, Over-round

Overlay

Odds laid by a bookmaker which seem to underestimate the winning chance of a contender.
See Value

Over-round

Term signifying that a set of odds for an event contains an element of potential profit for the bookmaker.
See Odds, Over-broke

Overstaking

Overstaking occurs where the total amount of stake money received by the bookmaker exceeds the amount required to execute a multiple bet to the specified unit stake. This error is resolved by returning the excess to the client after all the selections have run.
See Understaking

Owner's selected

Term used to select owner's preferred runner where two or more in the same ownership are running in the same race – deemed to be whichever starts at the shortest price. If two or more share the same shortest price, the stake is divided between them.

Pari-mutuel

French term (= mutual wager) used in many countries, including the United States, for the system of racecourse pool betting which, in Britain, we call a 'tote'. Strictly speaking, the tote (or 'totalisator') is the machinery used for recording the numbers of tickets sold.

Pari-mutuel betting originated in France in 1872. The first totalisator device was a hand-operated calculating machine used for a pari-mutuel in New Zealand in 1880.

When British bookmakers bet on race meetings in countries where there is no on-course bookmaking (such as the United States and France), settlement is usually according to the official pari-mutuel dividends. However, for some important events, British bookmakers lay their own 'list' prices. The two methods are capable of resulting in quite different odds so would-be bettors should satisfy themselves in advance that their bookmakers are prepared to lay their bet by the preferred method.

Table of combinations

Total number from which selections are to be made	Number of selections								
	Any 2	Any 3	Any 4	Any 5	Any 6	Any 7	Any 8	Any 9	Any 10
1									
2	1								
3	3	1							
4	6	4	1						
5	10	10	5	1					
6	15	20	15	6	1				
7	21	35	35	21	7	1			
8	28	56	70	56	28	8	1		
9	36	84	126	126	84	36	9	1	
10	45	120	210	252	210	120	45	10	1
11	55	165	330	462	462	330	165	55	11
12	66	220	495	792	924	792	495	220	66
13	78	286	715	1287	1716	1716	1287	715	286
14	91	364	1001	2002	3003	3432	3003	2002	1001
15	105	455	1365	3003	5005	6435	6435	5005	3003
16	120	560	1820	4368	8008	11440	12870	11440	8008
17	136	680	2380	6188	12376	19448	24310	24310	19448
18	153	816	3060	8568	18564	31824	43758	48620	43758
19	171	969	3876	11628	27132	50388	75582	92378	92378
20	190	1140	4845	15504	38760	77520	125970	167960	184756

Parlay

A 'parlay' (noun) is an American word for a double, treble or other accumulative bet. 'To parlay' (verb) means to re-invest the return from one bet in another bet.

Patent

Popular multiple bet consisting of 7 wagers from 3 selections: 3 singles, 3 doubles, and 1 treble. The singles ensure a return even if only one selection succeeds. Also known, less commonly, as a Twist.

Patent staking ready reckoner 3 selections 7 wagers 3 singles/3 doubles/1 treble					
Stake	Win	Each-way	Stake	Win	Each-way
0.05	0.35	0.70	0.55	3.85	7.70
0.10	0.70	1.40	0.60	4.20	8.40
0.15	1.05	2.10	0.65	4.55	9.10
0.20	1.40	2.80	0.70	4.90	9.80
0.25	1.75	3.50	0.75	5.25	10.50
0.30	2.10	4.20	0.80	5.60	11.20
0.35	2.45	4.90	0.85	5.95	11.90
0.40	2.80	5.60	0.90	6.30	12.60
0.45	3.15	6.30	0.95	6.65	13.30
0.50	3.50	7.00	1.00	7.00	14.00

Permutation

Strictly speaking, a 'permutation' consists of the ways of arranging a number of items or selection of items, *where different serial order counts as a different way.* There is a permutation, for instance, when the bettor makes a number of selections from a given race to be arranged in every possible way in forecasts. Thus, from 3 selections (A,B,C) there are 6 forecast permutations (AB, AC, BA, BC, CA, and CB).

How to find number of permutations or combinations

● The number of *permutations* is given by the following formula:

$$\frac{n!}{(n-r)!}$$

where n = total number from which selections are being made; r = number of selections forming each group; and $n!$ indicates 'n factorial', the product of all positive integers from 1 to n (thus, $3! = 1 \times 2 \times 3 = 6$).

● The number of *combinations*, where serial order does not count as a different way, is given by the following formula:

$$\frac{n!}{r!(n-r)!}$$

● The number of wagers in an accumulative bet in which more than one selection is made in each race is found by the product of the number of selections in each leg. Thus, in a treble in which there are 3 alternative selections in the first race, 2 selections in the second race, and 1 selection in the third race, the total would be $3 \times 2 \times 1$ bets = 6 bets.

But in betting, especially football betting, the term 'permutation' or 'perm' is used loosely to mean a betting plan covering all the possible doubles (or trebles, or fourfolds and so on) from a given larger number of selections. Such arrangements, where serial order does not count as a separate way, are properly known as 'combinations'. Thus, from a total of 3 selections in different events (A,B,C), there are 3 doubles (AB, AC, and BC).

It can be seen that, where serial order counts, there are more bets.

Photo-finish

Where the finish of a race is very close, the judge consults the evidence of the photo-finish camera before declaring a result. In the short interval before the order of finish is given, racecourse bookmakers may bet on the result. The odds are often very over-round or sometimes only one runner is offered, the probable loser.

Pitch

Allotted place in the betting ring at a racecourse where a

bookmaker sets up his 'joint'.
See Joint

Place betting

Place-only bets are not normally allowed in betting shops (except occasionally at Tote odds as described below). But subject to stipulations about numbers of runners, place bets may be made provided an equal amount is staked to win. These are called 'each-way' bets.

However, place-only betting facilities are provided by the totes at racecourses and greyhound tracks. Being a relatively easy bet, the dividends are not large but the bettor has the satisfaction of more frequent payouts than those betting in other pools!

Tote Bookmakers Ltd and some betting shops licensed to bet at Tote odds accept place-only bets at Tote odds, usually only in singles.

Placepot

See Placepot (greyhound), Tote Placepot

Placepot (greyhound)

A greyhound placepot, as offered by some betting shops, is a starting price place accumulator on 6 consecutive greyhound races (BAGS meetings only).

To succeed, the bettor must select a placed greyhound in each of the nominated races, the following being the place criteria and terms of settlement:

8 runners	1–2–3	$\frac{1}{4}$ SP odds
5, 6 or 7 runners	1–2	$\frac{1}{3}$ SP odds
4 or fewer	1	Win SP odds

Un-named first favourites are accepted. Permutations are allowed.

Pointspread

See Spread

Political betting

Election betting of a kind was offered by a bookmaker as long ago as 1935, but the betting proposition, a form of 'spread-betting' on the size of the majority, was a difficult one for bettors to grasp. In any event, in those pre-betting shop days, off-course wagering was circumscribed by many difficulties.

The seeds of modern election betting were sown in 1959 when Ron Pollard, the guru of political betting, along with a colleague at

William Hill, experimented with a method of election forecasting. For Pollard, it was a dry run but, in that same year, Ladbrokes (whom he subsequently joined) unwittingly hit the headlines of the *Daily Express* after making a telephone bet with Peter O'Sullevan at 4/6 the Conservatives. The significance of that event was that it indicated the power of political events to put betting odds, and the names of bookmakers, on to the front pages of newspapers.

Pollard was deeply interested in politics but the publicity value of political betting was undoubtedly a powerful influence persuading Ladbrokes, in 1963, to allow him to open a book on the election of a new leader for the Conservative Party, to replace Harold Macmillan. Ladbrokes took £14,000 on the event (a not inconsiderable amount in those days) and won £1,400. For the record, the winner was Sir Alec Douglas-Home, who entered the betting at 16/1 as a doubtful runner.

The publicity was enormous and political betting had undoubtedly arrived!

Today, it is possible to bet on the outcome of a General Election at any time. Because of the volatility of the electorate and the many ups-and-downs in the popularity of a party in power during the life of a Parliament, it is often possible to hedge a bet on one major party with a bet on the other at another time, guaranteeing a return. However, the bettor should take care that the bets are struck on like terms.

At General Elections there are odds for individual constituencies and odds for majorities, as well as outright betting. During the course of a Parliament, fiercely contested by-elections also often turn into horse races. Another area of betting which arouses keen interest, is the date of a forthcoming General Election. And in 1990, over one million pounds was staked overall on the outcome of the bitter Conservative Party leadership contest.

Political betting opportunities are by no means limited to domestic politics, the major bookmakers making a lively market in the outcome of the US presidential elections, for example.

Obviously, opinion polls are an important form pointer, but since these are instantly available to bookmaker and bettor alike, their findings are always likely to be discounted in the odds. The trick of election betting (insider information aside!) is to be able to look ahead, in particular to anticipate good or bad economic events – these seem to have a greater overall effect on voter sentiment than any other issue – capable of altering the appeal of the parties.

Those interested to read more about this fascinating subject will find the following books useful:

Richard Kaye, *The Ladbrokes Story*, London 1969 (out-of-print)

Ron Pollard, *Odds & Sods*, London 1991

The Sporting Life Guide to How to Pick Winners (Edited by David Bennett), London 1991 (contains an article about politics from a betting point of view 'Politics: you bet – the country decides' by Rob Hartnett of Ladbrokes).

See Fringe betting

Pool betting

In Britain, pool betting is known as 'Tote betting' (with a capital 'T'), as operated at horse race meetings by the Horserace Totalisator Board, or 'tote betting' (with a small 't'), as operated at greyhound tracks by each track promoter. In pool betting, the total stake money taken for a given class of bet in a given race is the 'pool' and the winnings are an equitable share of the pool after a deduction (or 'retention') by the promoter for operating costs and profit.

In many other countries, including major horse racing ones such as the United States and France, pool betting is the norm. In Britain, pool betting operates alongside, and competes for custom with, bookmakers, who are individual private traders.

The fundamental difference between bookmaking and pool betting is that, in the former case, the odds are controlled by the bookmaker, whereas in pool betting the odds are solely determined by the collective money and choices of those participating in the pool.

The bettor should not lose sight of the fact that a bet, on entering the pool, may have the effect of lowering the dividend. In a strong pool, the effect for most racegoers, betting average amounts, may be trivial. But in the case of a very large bet or, in a weak pool (such as the place pool at a thinly attended greyhound meeting), even a modest bet can sometimes cause the payout odds to plunge, to the dismay of the unwitting bettor. The following is a useful rule-of-thumb. For stakes of 2% of the total pool and less, for runners at odds of 3/1 and less, the bettor has little to fear from a diminished dividend as a result of his own bet.

Promoters of pool betting usually offer a variety of wagers, including carry-forward pools offering large payouts for small stakes, not available from on-course bookmakers.

See Tote

Postponement

Where a race is postponed and run later in the day, bets made prior to the announcement stand for the rearranged time. But most firms will cancel the bet, if so requested by the bettor before the rearranged time.

In the case of ante-post wagers, the bet stands until the post-poned race takes place. If the race is abandoned, the bettor's stake is returned.

Price

The payout-odds offered by a bookmaker about a runner.
See Odds

Probability

A 'probability' is the likelihood of an event occurring. Mathematically, it is expressed as a number on a scale of 0 (= 'no likelihood') to 1 (= 'certainty'). An 'even' chance on this scale is the midpoint 0.500. In betting, it is more usual to state probabilities as *percentages*, where the scale is 0 (= 'no likelihood') to 100 (= 'certainty'). This latter scale has disadvantages but it will be used here to conform to conventional usage. (To convert from one scale to another, multiply or divide by 100, as appropriate.)

'Odds' are another way of expressing probabilities, although it should not be imagined that the odds offered by bookmakers represent probabilities. They do not. Bookmakers' odds are merely the terms on which the bookmaker promises to settle a bet.

There are two ways of calculating probabilities with a degree of precision. Although neither method has a direct application to horse race and other sports betting situations, an understanding of them is required for a deeper insight of the underlying principles of betting.

(1) Probability from symmetry

In cases where, by virtue of symmetry, all the possible outcomes have the same likelihood of occurring (as, for example, the faces of a die or the slots of a gambling wheel), the probability of any outcome can be known exactly from the following formula:

$$\text{probability} = \frac{\text{number of favourable outcomes}}{\text{total number of outcomes}}$$

Thus, the probability of throwing a 'six' with a die is 1/6 (1 favourable outcome divided by 6 possible outcomes) = 0.167 (16.7%). And, the probability of throwing an odd number is 3/6 (3 favourable outcomes divided by 6 possible outcomes) = 0.500 (50.0%).

(2) Probability from repetition

In the cases of events which are not symmetrical but which are exactly repeatable, the approximate probability of the different outcomes can be found by a prolonged series of repetitions. In such a series of repetitions, the occurrences of each possible outcome are counted, giving the 'frequency of occurrence' of each outcome. The *approximate* probability of a selected outcome is given by the 'relative frequency':

$$\text{relative frequency} = \frac{\text{frequency of occurrence of selected outcome}}{\text{total number of repetitions}}$$

Relative frequency is not a reliable indicator of probability if the series of repetitions is a short one. As the number of repetitions increases, so the precision increases.

The method of relative frequency can be tested by applying it to a case in which probability is known from symmetry, such as 'heads' in a coin-spinning game $(1/2 = 0.500 = 50.0\%)$. In an actual experiment, the following were the relative frequencies of 'heads' after the given number of repetitions:

Repetitions	Occurrences of 'heads'	Relative frequency
10	6	0.600 (60.0%)
100	48	0.480 (48.0%)
1000	501	0.501 (50.1%)

If the method of relative frequencies is applied to events which are *similar* but not the same, the resulting relative frequency is not the probability of any individual case but an average of all the

---

The rules of multiplication and addition of probabilities

Within whatever limitation is imposed by the method by which an estimate of probability is reached, statements of probability of whatever kind can be worked with according to the same rules:

To find the probability of a combination of 2 or more unrelated events: Multiply together the separate probabilities. Thus, the probability of throwing an odd number in each of 3 consecutive rolls of a die is $1/2 \times 1/2 \times 1/2 = 1/8$ (12.5%).

To find the probability of the occurrence of two or more events which are mutually exclusive (that is to say, where the occurrence of one event debars the occurrence of the other): Add the probabilities of the events. Thus, the probability of throwing a 'one' or 'three' or 'five' in a single roll of a die is $1/6 + 1/6 + 1/6 = 3/6 = 1/2$ (50.0%).

individual probabilities. However, the more similar the events, the closer average probability and individual probability become. Thus, the relative frequency of 'heads' (after a suitably long series of repetitions) converges with the probability of each individual case as given by symmetry.

Horse races and other sports contests are neither symmetrical nor exactly repeatable, nor, in most cases, even very similar. Nevertheless, statements are freely made about supposed chances, usually in odds form. What is going on?

What pass for estimates of probability in the world of racing and sports betting are not probabilities at all. They are pseudo-probabilities, sometimes known as 'subjective probabilities'. They look like 'real' probabilities because the same odds (or sometimes percentage) notations are used. If a person states that Monica Seles is a 5/2 chance to win the French Open, the statement at face value has the appearance of an authoritative mathematical calculation. In fact, Seles' 'true' chance is known only to nature and the statement is merely an opinion, how good an opinion depending, as we shall see, upon the information available and the knowledge and freedom from bias of the person making the opinion.

The distinction between 'subjective probabilities' and 'real' probabilities is an important one because subjective probabilities can take a range of values, from individual to individual, whereas a 'real' probability has only one value, even though that value is known only to nature.

The different values assigned by different individuals is a function of (1) the state of information available to the individual, (2) the individual's accumulated knowledge and experience of the sport, and (3) the individual's emotional biases. The more complete the information, the more experienced and knowledgeable the person forming the opinion, the more free that person of any bias, so the more it is valid to regard the subjective probability as an approximation of a 'real' – though unknown – probability.

Likewise, the more defective is an opinion, from any of those three viewpoints, the less valid a subjective probability is likely to be. In betting and the estimation of probabilities, as in life, emotion has the power of overwhelming and contradicting reason. Thus, an individual, no matter how well-informed and knowledgeable, is capable of making a poor prediction if emotional bias is playing a part in the opinion-forming process.

The goal of the value-hunting bettor is therefore to maximise in himself the qualities which tend towards the soundest judgements: that is to say, acquire insight into the finer points of a chosen sport, become knowledgeable about its players, and remain coldly objective.

Fed the appropriate information, the brain does its work of inductive reasoning without conscious effort. (It is usually harder to *resist* forming an opinion than to have one!) Even so, the brain is not a digital computer outputting numbers. Language is its medium and opinions come in verbal form. If desired, verbal opinions can be placed on a scale and translated into numerical equivalents (one scheme for two-sided events is suggested in the panel below). This is a useful exercise for testing the plausibility of an opinion, especially while the bettor is honing his skills. But in due course, the brain tends to assimilate that function too, so that anomalous odds tend to stand out.

One final point. It is unrealistic to try to discriminate very fine intervals. Anyone who believes a runner to be a 6/4 chance and good value at 13/8 is deceiving himself! Likewise, the differences between such odds as 16/1 (5.9%) and 25/1 (3.8%) and 50/1 (2.0%), although apparently large when expressed in odds form,

---

Suggested numerical equivalents for different degrees of verbal conviction in 2-sided events

Verbal estimate of chance of Side A	Numerical value for Side A	Numerical value for Side B
'equal'	50.0% (1/1)	50.0%(1/1)
'better'	55.6% (4/5)	44.4% (5/4)
'much better'	66.7% (1/2)	33.3% (2/1)
'mismatch'	80.0% (1/4)	20.0% (4/1)

Note: the sum of the values for Sides A and B is always 100% (= 'certainty')

---

are in reality small, as the percentages show, and must be considered indiscriminable. The value-seeking bettor is only looking for margins which are palpable.

As there are no means whereby the bettor can tell, on a given occasion, whether an assigned subjective probability is correct, success or failure can only be known from long-term results.

See Odds, Value

Psychology of betting

In life, everyone gambles occasionally. Successes do not come without cost and the risk of failure. Since Mrs Grundy was married, it is evident she too gambled on at least one occasion!

Gambling, in order to improve one's situation in life, is unavoidable. But betting on the outcome of races is different. It is self-inflicted. Why should a person voluntarily expose himself to the anxiety of a risky speculation and the possibility of loss?

Somebody who has never experienced the elation that follows a seemingly gratuitous gain would not be able to understand. But, for those who have ever tasted, the flavour is unforgettable. To taste again, one must bet again. But the elation has a dark side too. To experience the pleasure of winning, one must also endure the sting of losing. How does one dispel the disappointment that follows a losing bet? . . . With hope, in the form of the next race on the card.

It is thus a curious characteristic of betting (and one to which the bookmaking industry owes its profitable existence) that both winning and losing bring on the desire to do the same thing: to bet again. After winning, to re-create the excitement. After losing, to try to wipe out the sense of loss. So, in a chain reaction, the process continues, win or lose, until outside circumstances, like the end of the race meeting, bring it to a halt.

Betting for many people, then, is a game played with the emotions. In a well-adjusted individual, it is harmless and relaxing. Those who play the betting game to excess do so because excess is already written into their personalities.

However, betting as an emotional response to the preceding bet is unlikely to lead one on to the course of profit. The few who manage, in the long term, to take out of betting more than they put into it are drawn from the ranks of another group. Those who have struggled with their emotions and achieved a degree of self-regulation.

For such persons, betting is a battle. The odds are an adversary to be defeated. Predicting the outcome of a race is a problem for the intellect. The net win or loss from an individual meeting is not a cause either for joy or despondency but a statistical occurrence.

Achieving control over the emotions does not in itself make betting profitable but it is an essential state of mind if the problem is to be tackled at all.

Without the participation of those who bet purely for excitement or other emotional payoff, bettors of the more rational variety would not have a game worth playing. Willy-nilly, the promoters, bookmakers or totalisator, are going to take their percentage out of the betting turnover. Therefore, for some bettors to get a better-than-average return requires that other bettors get a worse-than-average return.

It is worth considering what worse-than-average betting means. Bettors who apply a random or superstitious method to selection, such as sticking with a pin or betting on the basis of lucky numbers, are *not* worse-than-average bettors. Their random technique ensures a balance of good and bad value. They are truly *average* bettors. To qualify as worse-than-average requires *negative* wisdom: that is to say, a process of decision-making which runs counter to what is sensible and wise.

It is known statistically that (in horse and greyhound racing, at least) runners at longer odds make a bigger contribution to the bookmakers' take-out than shorter-priced runners. In other words, when bettors back longshots, they grossly overestimate their likelihood of succeeding and bookmakers are able to lay much unfairer odds than they can about the favourites. It is this phenomenon which enhances the possibility of finding value at the shorter end of the book. The reasoning that underlies the behaviour of a betting crowd is very hard to fathom, but one can nevertheless speculate as to what might be the pressures which encourage bettors to wager on runners with only a small chance of winning without a proper consideration of the odds they should get in return for the risk:

(1) **The lure of a big payout for a modest stake.** The bettor reasons that, because only a small sum is put at risk, the bet is a prudent one. Not so. The same small stake, wagered on favourites, could be expected to yield a far better return.

(2) **A dislike of odds-on wagers, where the winnings are less than the sum put at risk.**

(3) **The desire to recoup losses.** After a run of losers, the bettor may be overwhelmed by the desire to recover prior losses. With a diminished capital and only a few betting opportunities remaining, he may, fatally, look to outsiders as a means of getting even.

(4) **The underdog effect.** Some people just cannot help, for

emotional reasons, betting on the underdog. Since the contender who is the underdog reaps no personal benefit from the wagers he or she carries, the behaviour is all the more irrational!

The psychology of betting is a complex and intriguing subject, only touched on here, and one which has not been very well explained by those who heretofore have tried to study it. Many so-called 'explanations' of betting behaviour have been formulated by individuals with an anti-betting agenda. Such investigators are attracted by anecdotal forms of evidence based around persons who have gambled to excess, which of course excludes the majority who are individuals betting well within their limits for the fun and relaxation it provides. To utter 'I bet you' is a totally normal human impulse and those who presumptuously characterise betting as an unworthy form of behaviour merely advertise their own suspect state of mind and dubious motives.

See Utility

Punter

Client of a bookmaker or betting shop. The term, which is at least 250 years old, originally denoted a player at a gaming house (*ie* casino). Its use as a term to describe one who bets on horse races was established by about 1880.

Push

American term for a tied bet. In the United States, it is customary to cancel such bets and return stakes to the bettor.

Racecourse betting

At a race meeting, horse or greyhound, the bettor can choose between betting with the tote or bookmakers.

Totes offer several bets (place only, forecasts etc) not available from bookmakers.

The battleground between tote and bookmaker is the straight win bet. Most very large bets go to bookmakers since to wager an amount out of proportion to the total in the tote pool is a self-defeating exercise in winning back one's own money. The strength of a pool obviously depends by and large on the attendance at the meeting. As a rule-of-thumb, it is not advisable to stake an amount greater than 2% of the total in the win pool if one is backing a favourite, or $\frac{1}{2}$% for second and third favourites.

However, for the vast majority of bettors there is a real choice between the 'firm' odds offered by the bookmakers and the dividend of the tote, which is subject to fluctuations until every stake is in the pool and the result of the race known.

It is great fun shopping for 'prices' among the bookmakers. Occasionally one will succeed in getting the best offered, but on average over the long term, this is an unattainable ideal. It is generally good policy to bet shortly before the 'off' when the over-round (see 'Odds', p. 69) is most favourable. But an even more important consideration for the bettor must be the overall amount of over-round to which the bookmakers are betting.

The Tote (horse racing) makes a fixed deduction from the win pool of 16%, approximately the equivalent of a 'book' of 119.

The *maximum* tote retention permitted at greyhound tracks is 29%, roughly equivalent to a 'book' of 141. However, the retention is likely to vary from pool to pool and be much less for the 'win' pool. The racegoer at a given track is urged to consult the notices, specifying the deductions, posted near totalisator windows.

Bookmakers are ever eager to take racegoers' money but, for the newcomer, the brash self-assurance of the layers can be off-putting.

The way to make a bet is to walk up to the bookmaker of one's choice, first making sure no other is offering the selection on better terms. State the runner clearly by name, state the amount to be staked, and state the displayed odds. The bookmaker relays the instruction to his clerk, sometimes translating it into a jargon of his own: 'Heatwave ... three fivers to one' which means a £5 bet on Heatwave at odds of 3/1.

The racegoer, after a while, gradually learns to make his requests for bets in the same form as the bookmaker but, so long as the instruction is clear and unambiguous, the bookmaker is happy to receive bets in plain English. Many bookmakers tape-record while taking bets, so that there is a record of a transaction in the event of a dispute. If a dispute at a horse race meeting cannot be settled, a Ring Inspector is available after each race to help resolve the situation and give advice.

The bookmaker, for his part, gives the bettor a thick card ticket bearing a number. It carries no details of the bet. At first, this is a little unsettling, but the racegoer soon learns to have confidence that winning bets will be settled satisfactorily.

If the selection wins the race, the bettor joins the queue of other fortunate investors waiting for the bookmaker to open his satchel. When his turn to collect arrives, he should tender his ticket and state the amount he expects to be paid (including the original stake). In the case of the £5 bet on Heatwave at 3/1, the bettor would claim £20 consisting of £15 in winnings plus the returned stake of £5. The bookmaker checks the amount with his clerk and, providing both parties are in agreement, he tears up the ticket and pays out the required sum.

Not the least of the attractions of going to the racecourse to bet is that on-course wagers are not liable to government Betting Duty.

In addition to the betting facilities at horse race meetings provided by the Tote and bookmakers, there is usually a betting shop giving a service along conventional betting shop lines (see 'NARBOL', p. 66), including bets on other meetings and the afternoon's greyhound racing.

Bettors can also wager on other horse race meetings, deduction-free, with the 'away' bookmakers in the Ring, either at board prices or SP.

See NARBOL, Odds, Tote betting on-course

Racing rules (RR)

Patrons of betting shops which customarily operate 'first past the post' settlement who prefer the option of settlement according to the official result (*ie* after any objection or enquiry) should mark their betting slip 'racing rules' or 'RR'.

See First past the post

Rails bookmakers

Racecourse bookmakers occupying privileged positions along the rails separating the Members' enclosure from Tattersalls enclosure. They are thus able to trade with clients in the Members' enclosure in which bookmakers are not permitted to stand. Rails bookmakers are considered an elite among bookmakers.

Related contingencies

A contingency is the event upon which the outcome of a bet is determined – reaching the winning line first, scoring more goals than the opposing side, and so on.

Two or more contingencies can only be linked as a double or accumulator at multiplied odds if the contingencies are *independent* – that is to say, if the result of one part is unaffected by the result of another part.

Where the result of one of the contingencies has a bearing on the chance of another, say a 'correct score' and 'outright result' for the same football match, the contingencies are said to be *related*. In such cases, the odds can only be taken in singles.

Where doubles or accumulators are taken about related contingencies in error, the stake is equally divided and invested in the specified contingencies as single bets.

Re-runs

A greyhound race which has been declared void by the stewards may sometimes be re-run at the end of the meeting. For the purpose of settling, a re-run is deemed to have the same race number and racetime as the no-race of which it is a re-run. In other words, the 1.22 pm is still known as the first race and the 1.22, even if it is re-run at 5.00 at the end of the card.

Bets for the original race stand for the re-run unless cancelled by mutual consent before the re-run takes place. If the race is re-run with fewer runners, bets on the withdrawn greyhounds are void with stakes returnable.

Where a 'show price' has been taken on the original race, settlement reverts to SP for the re-run.

Reserves

In greyhound racing, the place of a withdrawn greyhound is sometimes taken by a reserve, if the withdrawal is known before the meeting begins. Every effort is made to inform betting shop clients of the substitution.

Unless a bettor wishes to be on a trap number, come what may, selections are best specified by name. Selections specified by number alone are on that trap even if a reserve runs in place of the scheduled runner. If both name and number are given, name takes precedence, and the bettor is on a non-runner if a reserve runs from that trap.

Reserve greyhounds are often under-rated by the odds and this is an area where value can often be found.

Return

The sum due from the bookmaker on winning or void betting slips. A winning return consists of stake+winnings, less tax (10% of the total amount) if tax has not been prepaid. A £5 bet on a winner at 3/1, for example, settles as follows:

> **Tax prepaid**
> Stake £5 *plus* Winnings 3×£5 = Return £20
>
> **Tax not prepaid**
> Stake and Winnings of £20 (as above) *less* £2 tax
> (£20×10/100) = Return £18

In the case of void bets, stakes are returned in full, without deduction.

The sum of all of a bettor's returns divided by total money staked and expressed as a percentage is a useful and easily maintained statistic by which a bettor is able to monitor his own performance. Calculate thus:

$$\% \text{ return} = \frac{\text{total returns (winnings incl. stakes, } \textit{less} \text{ any tax)}}{\text{total money staked}} \times 100$$

Thus, a bettor whose aggregated returns during the course of a year are £842 for an expenditure in stakes of £1,040 (£20 per week), has an overall return of 81%, a loss of 19%. A bettor whose aggregated returns are £1,082 for an expenditure in stake money of £1,040 has an overall return of 104%, a gain of 4%.

See Tax

How to calculate a return at any odds

(1) Convert odds, if necessary, to odds-to-1 by dividing the lefthand figure by the righthand figure (a calculator helps): $9/2 = 4.5/1$

(2) Ignore righthand figure (*ie* 1): 4.5

(3) Multiply by stake (say, £5): £22.50. These are the *winnings*

(4) Add original stake (£5): £27.50. This is the *return* (*ie* winnings+stake)

(5) To deduct betting tax of 10%, multiply amount found by Step 4 by 0.90: £24.75

(6) To calculate place return to ¼ odds, multiply amount in Step 3 by 0.20: £4.50. Add stake (£5): £9.50. If betting tax of 10% is liable, multiply by 0.90: £8.55

(7) To calculate place return to ¼ odds, multiply amount in Step 3 by 0.25: £5.62. Add stake (£5): £10.62. If betting tax of 10% is liable, multiply by 0.90: £9.56

Reverse forecast

Simple form of permutation combining 2 selections (A, B) in 2 forecasts (AB, BA). The bet requires 2 stakes and wins if the selections finish 1st and 2nd in either order.

A dual-forecast, available at horse race meetings from the Tote and at some betting shops off-course, gives the same cover for a single stake.

See Dual-forecast

Rigged betting

In a betting context, to 'rig' means artificially to manipulate betting odds with a view to making an unfair gain.

Bookmakers now reserve the right, in cases where there is evidence of price rigging, to declare such a contest void for betting purposes and to treat as a non-runner a selection which is included in an accumulative bet.

One of the most celebrated cases of price-rigging was the so-called 'Dagenham coup', attempted at the now defunct East London greyhound track in 1964.

By monopolising all the tote windows, the organisers successfully contrived matters so that there was just one winning tote unit, paying a staggering dividend of £987 11s 9d, odds of nearly 10,000/1. Accomplices off-course had placed bets which would have netted an estimated £10 million – if bookmakers had paid out. Some bookmakers did make ex gratia payments, while others settled on the basis of an estimated 'fair' dividend, but most declared the race void for betting purposes, returning stakes to winners and losers alike.

Ring

Collective term for the bookmakers in a given enclosure at the race-course. The Ring (capital 'R') is the main betting ring in the enclosure known as Tattersalls. The bookmakers in the next lower enclosure are called the 'Silver Ring'.

Ring Inspector

Jockey Club official, in attendance at race meetings, available to help resolve cases of disputed bets and, if necessary, advise the parties of their right to refer to Tattersalls Committee. The point where the Ring Inspector can be found after each race is designated by a notice.

Roll-up

An accumulator.
See Accumulator

Roundabout

Consists of 3 singles on 3 selections (A,B,C) with 'any-to-come' doubles at two times the original stake on the other two, thus:

> £2 win A any-to-come £4 double BC
> £2 win B any-to-come £4 double AC
> £2 win C any-to-come £4 double AB

The 'any-to-come' bets are technically separate wagers so that, even if tax has been prepaid on the singles, any return arising from the

any-to-come elements is liable to further tax.
See Rounder

Rounder

Consists of 3 singles on 3 selections (A,B,C) with 'any-to-come' doubles at the same stake on the other two, thus:

> £2 win A any-to-come £2 double BC
> £2 win B any-to-come £2 double AC
> £2 win C any-to-come £2 double AB

The 'any-to-come' bets are technically separate wagers so that, even if tax has been prepaid on the singles, any return arising from the any-to-come elements is liable to further tax.
See Roundabout

Round Robin

A wager of 10 bets consisting of 3 selections (A,B,C) in 3 doubles, 1 treble and each pair in single-stakes-about singles. Thus:

> 50p double AB
> 50p double AC
> 50p double BC
> 50p treble ABC
> 50p win A any-to-come 50p win B
> 50p win B any-to-come 50p win A
> 50p win A any-to-come 50p win C
> 50p win C any-to-come 50p win A
> 50p win B any-to-come 50p win C
> 50p win C any-to-come 50p win B

The 'any-to-come' bets are technically separate wagers so that, even if tax has been prepaid on the original bets, any return arising from the any-to-come elements is liable to further tax.
See Single-stakes-about, Stakes-about

Round-the-clock

Elaborate 'any-to-come' bet for 3 or more selections. Each selection is staked as a single, followed by any-to-come singles on the other selections rotating. Thus, for 3 selections (A,B,C):

> £2 win A any-to-come £2 win B any-to-come £2 win C
> £2 win B any-to-come £2 win C any-to-come £2 win A
> £2 win C any-to-come £2 win A any-to-come £2 win B

For larger numbers of selections, the same principle is followed.

The any-to-come bets are technically separate wagers, so that, even if tax has been prepaid on the original singles, any return arising from any-to-come elements is liable to further tax.

Ruin

'Ruin' is a technical term used by mathematicians who study gambling situations. It does not mean (hopefully) the loss of all of a person's worldly goods, but the loss of a given capital set aside for a gambling purpose.

In a favourable game, the probability of ruin decreases exponentially as starting capital increases (see, 'Frank Spitzer, *Principles of Random Walk*, 1964').

See Favourable game, Staking plans

Rule 4c

See Tattersalls Rule 4c

Satellite Information Services (SIS)

Satellite Information Services Ltd, the company that transmits betting shows, results and live television coverage of horse and greyhound racing to betting shops.

Address: Satellite Information Services Ltd, Satellite House, 17 Corsham Street, London N1 6DR. Telephone: 071-253 2232.

Screen price

Alternative term for 'show price', reflecting the use of television screens in modernised shops for transmitting information about the racing.

See Show price

Selection methods

The art of betting is not just about picking winners. After all, someone using a pin will, in the course of time, have their share – how many depending on the average size of the fields. In greyhound racing, for example, where most races involve 6 runners, the pin-wielding bettor can expect, in the long-term, an average strike-rate of one winner in six.

Although we may bet, first and foremost, for fun and entertainment, part of the enjoyment is trying to make a gain. We can greatly improve our chance of doing this if we focus our attention on finding winners at good average odds. To make a long-term gain, the greyhound bettor using a purely random method would need average odds greater than 5/1. But, in practice, he could only expect to achieve an average of between 7/2 and 4/1.

The same goes for all random methods of making selections – such as bets based on lucky numbers, coincidences and birth dates. Occasionally, someone using such a method will hit the jackpot – by luck – but generally speaking it is a method of betting which cannot be recommended.

The bettor who graduates from pin-sticking or other random method to a mode of selection taking into account the different abilities of the runners, can expect, by so doing, to attain a better strike-rate. However, with the improved frequency of winners comes (unfortunately!) a corresponding drop in average odds.

Let us suppose, for example, that the bettor makes his 'form' selection vicariously by 'following the favourite'. Staying with greyhound racing for our examples (although the same principle applies to horse racing), this could be expected to yield an average of one winner in three – a good strike-rate – but the average odds of those winners sinks to about 7/4, less than the 5/2 needed to show a gain.

So what can be done to improve one's chances and get a better return from one's betting?

Basically, one must learn to identify and restrict one's wagers to the 'good' bets. Such a bet is one in which the 'real' chance of the runner is greater than the chance suggested by the odds. A 'bad' bet, vice versa. Clearly, betting on runners with a 6/4 chance at odds of 2/1 will lead to a little profit, while betting on 2/1 chances at odds of 6/4 will lead to loss.

When a bet is struck at odds better than the odds representing the runner's natural chance, the odds are said to contain 'value'. Whatever method of selection is adopted, it cannot be successful unless the principle of finding value is adhered to.

How useful to the bettor are the tips of newspaper experts? As with other methods of selection based upon following the opinions of others (such as backing favourites or reacting to 'market moves'), the bettor is likely to be acting in concert with a large body of other bettors, a fact which is bound to be reflected by the betting market. A good strike-rate may be attained but the average odds of a newspaper selector's winners, in the long term, are likely to be insufficient to pay for the losing selections. An analysis of the performance of newspaper greyhound tipsters, for example, showed an average strike-rate of 29% and average odds of 2/1, less than the 3/1 needed to show a gain. The very act of sharing their opinions with their readership has an influence upon the demand for bets and, through the mechanism of the betting market, that means lower odds.

However, newspaper correspondents are not without their usefulness! Because the betting market tends to be affected by what the experts are saying, value sometimes appears in *another* selection when the most influential of the tipsters all select the same runner, leading to too much support and bad value. Alternatively, a trusted tipster 'on his own' may supply a good value winner. For horse racing, there is a greater range of tipsters, so that the horse racing betting public is less polarised. Like greyhound tipsters, they tend to succeed on about 29% of occasions, although some attain better average odds than others.

One way to find value is to develop one's own skill in reading form – and then to follow one's own judgement, regardless of the market and newspaper selections. Not only is this satisfying – it can actually pay off in terms of better average odds. Nevertheless, there are many who want to bet – sensibly – but who simply do not have time to follow form at first hand. The bettor who wants to follow expert opinion should read and assimilate the views of more than one writer and, bearing in mind that such experts do not control the odds at which their selections start, the bettor himself should take responsibility for deciding if the odds are favourable.

Finally, of what value is 'information'?

It is only to be expected that those closest to a runner (its 'connections') are well placed to know a little of its fitness and potential in the days leading up to the race. They may feel sufficiently enthusiastic to risk a sizeable bet.

In betting, as in the stock market, information translated into money is communicated very rapidly. The price of a gambled-on runner tumbles in proportion to the money staked and lack of countervailing investments in any other runner in the field. Bettors on hand at the race meeting or in the betting shop may be tempted to follow the market down with a bet of their own on the gambled-on runner. Sometimes such gambles succeed – although, for the average bettor, the payoff odds are diminished in value by the cuts in price which have to take place before the bettor realises something is afoot.

The worth of so-called 'inside information' should not be over-estimated. However much a runner's connections may know about their own runner, they are not equally well-informed about the other contenders in the field. And so-called information is made up of unwisdom as well as wisdom. For the bettor, it is necessarily difficult to discriminate between good judgement and what may be no more than over-enthusiasm. The bettor is better off concentrating on the form book which, notwithstanding any occasional behind-the-scenes manoeuvring, is the source of most winners.

Settler

Betting shop employee responsible for checking the betting slips and calculating the returns due.

Show

State of the betting at the racecourse at a given point in time. As in 'first show', meaning the odds put up by a bookmaker when the betting opens.

Show pool

Name used by pari-mutuels in the United States for the 1-2-3 pool. There is a separate place pool which is for 1-2 only. This creates problems of interpretation in the case of each-way bets in Britain on American racing. *The Sporting Life* takes the view that, unless the bettor stipulates 1-2 on the betting slip, each-way bets on American racing should be interpreted as 'win and show' (*ie* 1-2-3).

Show price

The odds at which betting shop bets are normally settled are determined by the betting market on the course. In the period before a race – 2 or 3 minutes in the case of greyhounds, longer for horses – the prices being offered by the bookmakers at the track are transmitted to betting shops and displayed on a screen (or handwritten on printed lists) against the name of each runner. The display is updated as fluctuations in the odds occur. Odds are shortened or lengthened depending on the supply and demand for bets at the course.

These odds transmitted from the racecourse are called 'show prices'.

The customer who is following the action in the betting shop has the option, for 'single' bets, of taking the current 'show price', which must be specifically requested and noted and initialled on the betting slip by the counter clerk. Otherwise (with the exception of 'ante-post' or 'day-of-the-race' prices), racing bets are settled at 'starting prices' (or 'SP').

The question arises whether it is advantageous to take a 'show price'. It should be noted that the early shows from the racecourse bookmakers tend to be conservative ones. As trading gets under way, prices individually shorten and lengthen but *overall* they tend to relax and the 'over-round' (or potential margin of profit for the bookmaker) of the odds taken together is generally at its lowest at the time of the 'off'.

This would suggest that, on average over the long term, the bettor is better off not taking a show price – unless he has some special piece of information or insight suggesting that a selection will be backed-in as soon as the market opens.

See Bookmaker, Odds, Starting prices

Single

A 'single' – unlike a double or other form of accumulative bet – is not linked to any other bet.

The simplest and best-known of all is the 'win single', in which one runner is nominated to win the race. The bet is written on a plain betting slip and is settled at the appropriate odds if the runner finishes the race in first position. In an 'each-way single' (requiring 2 stakes), there is a return if the selection wins or is placed.

Single-stakes-about (S-S-A)

A bet consisting of 2 singles, each with an 'any-to-come' single at the same stake on the other selection. In effect, this doubles the stake on each selection if both win.

The any-to-come bets are technically separate wagers, so that, even if tax has been prepaid on the original bets, further tax is due on any return arising from the any-to-come elements.

A single-stakes-about bet is sometimes denoted by a cross or series of crosses between the selections (*eg* £2 A xxxxx £2 B). Hence, the alternative term 'cross bet' for this kind of wager.

See Double-stakes-about

Skinner

Racecourse bookmakers' slang for an unbacked winner.

Slang

As racecourse executives have modernised their operations and concentrated their minds on attracting the general consumer, so have gone many of the raffish, some would say colourful, aspects of racecourse culture. Part of that culture is the slang spoken by bookmakers and some other habitués of the betting rings – a curious amalgam of backslang, London slang and words unique to racing. Although still used, it has the aura of another generation about it, as if it is about to pass into history like the sticks of chalk with which bookmakers used to mark up prices on their boards.

Slang words used for round sums of money – 'score' (£20), 'pony' (£25), 'century' or 'ton' (£100), 'monkey' (£500), and 'grand' (£1,000) – are not peculiar to racing: 'pony' and 'monkey' seem to have their origin in gaming, but all the terms could equally be regarded as underworld, market trading, or even antique dealing as well as betting slang.

There is a whole repertoire of slang words for different odds, based on a mixture of rhyming slang, backslang and tic-tac signals, whose purpose was originally mainly to conceal information from the uninformed public. A few examples are 'Burlington Bertie' (rhyming slang) 100/30, 'neves' (backslang) 7/1, 'top of the head' (tic-tac) 9/4, and 'up the arm' (tic-tac) 11/8.

A few other notable words are: 'beeswax' or 'bees', betting tax; 'face' (see p. 34); 'flimp', underpay; 'jolly', favourite; 'levels', evens; 'mug' (see p. 64); 'nanny', Tote; 'rag', outsider; 'skinner', unbacked winner; 'tools', a board bookmaker's equipment; and 'thick' (of a bet), large.

Sleeper

Bookmakers' term for a betting slip on which a return is due but which remains unclaimed.

Speciality bet

A company's own-name bet, often offering bonuses and consolations, for which special printed slips are supplied. Speciality bets are usually governed by special rules, which are either printed on the slip itself or displayed in the shop.

Speciality bets are designed to market the most profitable (for the bookmaker) areas of betting shop business.

Split

Alternative name, used in some areas of the north, for a Round Robin.

Sports betting

By 'sports betting' is meant wagering on all those sports other than the traditional betting sports of horse and greyhound racing. Soccer (see p. 38), American football (see p. 16), rugby, golf, snooker, tennis, boxing, motorsport, cricket, athletics and darts are among the most prominent, but almost any high-profile live televised event is liable to arouse some betting interest. Because such sports are conducted independently of betting objectives, sports betting is more or less free of the manoeuvring and secrecy which tend to be a characteristic of racing.

Since many sports bettors are prone to wagering on a partisan basis, rather than on an objective viewpoint based on form, value (see p. 122) far exceeding anything that can be expected in horse or greyhound racing can often be found. In sports betting there are no SPs. Each bookmaking firm makes its own prices. By judiciously choosing from among them, the bettor, in effect, lessens the over-round. On occasions, the best of all the available prices may even be under-round.

General press coverage of the sports in question tends to be in the more lyrical, less objective, style suited to 'fans' rather than betting-oriented readers. Bettors are therefore urged to follow the sports betting coverage in the *Life* and to read specialised sports magazines to obtain background information in depth.

Advice and information about betting aspects of soccer, American football, golf, snooker, tennis, boxing, rugby and motorsport are given in 'The Sporting Life Guide to How to Pick Winners' (see p. 127).

Spread

'Spread' (in full, 'pointspread') is a term used in American football betting to denote the handicap points awarded the underdog in order to balance the apparent chances of the two sides. A team is said to 'cover the spread' (1) if, as favourite, it wins after conceding handicap points to the underdog, or (2) if, as underdog, it wins 'straight-up' or loses by a margin of points less than the handicap points awarded.

See American football, Handicap betting

Spread-betting

'Spread-betting' is a form of betting available from a limited number of specialised firms, through credit accounts. The use of the word 'spread' invites confusion with handicap spreads as encountered, for example, in American football betting. Spread-betting is something quite different.

In spread-betting, the bettor buys and sells 'positions', in the same way that financial or commodity 'futures' are bought and sold in the City of London. But in a betting context, the commodity which is traded are points, not coffee beans or Deutschmarks, the betting firm agreeing to sell a position to or buy a position from the bettor at the going rate at the time when the transaction is made. There is a margin of difference between selling and buying price, just as in financial markets, from which the bookmaker derives a profit. The fluctuations in buying and selling prices are determined by the unfolding of the sports event which is the basis of the bet.

For a specific example, let us take an imaginary market in the total number of points accumulated by, say, Arsenal, in the course of a football season. At a given point in the season, the bookmaker might be making a price of 75/77. A bettor expecting Arsenal to reach a point-score at the end of the season greater than 77 could buy points at 77 at, say, £10 per point. If Arsenal finished the season with 83 points, the bookmaker would settle as follows:

$$83 \text{ less } 77 = 6 \times £10 = £60 \text{ profit}$$

If, however, Arsenal finished with 71 points, settlement would be as follows:

$$77 \text{ less } 71 = 6 \times £10 = £60 \text{ loss}$$

The bettor has the option of selling a position, at whatever is the current selling rate. When the price stood at 75/77 the bettor could have sold for 75. In which case, settlement at the end of the season, if Arsenal finished with 71 points, would be as follows:

$$75 \text{ less } 71 = 4 \times £10 = £40 \text{ profit}$$

The prices available fluctuate throughout the course of a competition, according to the changing likelihood of the future outcome of the event. Clearly, spread-betting calls for constant vigilance on the part of the bettor, in order to get out of ('close') a deteriorating position.

Spreads are quoted for individual matches as well as events such as football league points which unfold slowly. Cricket matches, tennis matches and golf tournaments are examples of events which, by virtue of their volatility, lend themselves to spread-betting.

Spread-betting is an intriguing and different kind of betting experience – and one which calls for wariness and constant alertness!

Stake

The sum of money put at risk by a bettor.

How much should one stake per bet? That depends how many bets one plans to make in a period of time. Basically the total for a day or week or month should be no more than one can affordably lose entirely. In reality, of course, even at the very worst, one receives back in winnings a proportion of money staked. But winnings do not return at regular intervals or when they are required. So it is best to assume that all one's betting money is dedicated to entertainment purposes and is not required for the essentials of everyday living.

Because of the ever-present desire to win an amount sufficient to elicit from winning bets a feeling of real gain, there is always some psychological pressure occasionally to risk unaffordable sums. However, betting wisdom decrees that stakes should always be small in proportion to available resources. The person who can resist the temptation to stake beyond affordable limits, bets from a position of strength. For a wider discussion of the issues involved in forming a staking policy, refer to 'Staking plans' on p. 103.

See Staking plans

Stakes-about

A form of 'any-to-come' bet.
See Double-stakes-about, Single-stakes-about

Staking plans

A 'staking plan' usually means a scheme for increasing the stake at intervals in order to defeat, in theory, the effect of losing runs – by re-instating lost capital as soon as one or two winners are attained. In practice, sooner or later, a losing run comes along which is long enough to wipe out both staking plan and capital!

Schemes for incrementing stakes after losers are pointless because no scheme for varying stakes, no matter how ingenious, can, in the long term, alter the mathematical expectation of loss or gain. Level stakes, *ie* the same amount for every bet, is the best policy to follow.

Some staking plans recommend increasing the size of bet, not after losers, but after winners – on the proposition that this 'plays up winnings' by betting with 'their' (*ie* the bookmaker's) money.

But is the money really the bookmaker's? What about the bettor's prior losses? Whose money is that? Just as a shopkeeper must re-stock his shelves from the takings, so the prudent bettor needs to reinstate lost betting capital from successful bets.

It is worth noting that accumulative bets and some conditional bets are, in effect, self-contained though disguised staking plans which 'play up' winnings. Without detracting from the fun and hope that accumulative bets bring in exchange for small affordable initial stakes, one wonders whether bettors would be as insouciant about parlaying their winnings if each leg were re-staked on a bet-by-bet basis!

Some writers suggest increasing stakes when the apparent margin of value is greatest, the theory being that this gives the bettor a greater return on investment. But this is an over-hopeful view of the value-finding process – in the first place, over-estimating the *range* in the margin of value that is likely to be found and the degree to which differences in that range are likely to be discriminable, and, secondly, not admitting of inevitable occasional errors of judgement. The bettor is urged to take the statistical view that, by intelligently betting on those occasions when the odds *appear* to contain a margin of value, he can anticipate an actual margin of value *on average over the long term*. A level stake optimises the unknown ups-and-downs of individual bets.

In any event, it is a mathematical rule that, in a *favourable* game (see p. 35), the optimum bet is the smallest allowed by the rules since that minimises the possibility of the bettor being 'ruined', that is to say of encountering a run of bets that consumes the bettor's capital before the objective of a given increase in fortune is attained. In practice, most players are unable to operate the minimum stake rule because it comes into conflict with psychological pressures – in particular the desire for the excitement attendant upon taking a risk or of winning a large sum (see 'Utility, p. 122).

In the real world, therefore, it is clearly not always possible to follow mathematical truth wherever it may lead. To take account of psychological as well as mathematical criteria, it is reasonable to redefine an optimum bet as that amount greater than the minimum stake which is just sufficient to maintain interest. But, in any event, to obtain a reasonable amount of protection from a ruinous losing run, a bettor should, at the very most, stake no more than one-twentieth of a starting capital or, stated a different way, no more than one-twentieth of whatever sum the bettor feels he can lose before feeling regret. Of course, no amount of capital (except infinite capital!) can protect the bettor from 'ruin' if he is betting on 'unfavourable' terms (see below). Such a bettor is kept going solely by constantly drawing on new funds.

There are many bettors, otherwise wise in their betting decisions, whose undoing is to wager, given their resources, unaffordable amounts. A non-mathematical, psychological consequence of such unwise staking is the progressive effect of serial losses on the bettor's decision-making processes. A bettor may lose, say, £20 in the first race with equanimity. His bet on the next occasion may still be a rational one. However, the cumulative effect of each further loss without a win tends to bear down upon the bettor until he becomes overwhelmed by a desire to recoup losses. Therein lie the seeds of destruction if such feelings lead, as is likely, to less wise betting decisions.

In an *unfavourable* game, where the player does not expect to find a long-term margin of value and where betting is undertaken solely for such motives as entertainment and excitement, the minimum stake rule self-evidently need not apply since it is axiomatic that betting capital is inevitably eroded and be in constant need of replenishment. The only rule applicable here is that the bettor should stake the least amount necessary to yield the desired amount of pleasure, thus ensuring a given level of enjoyment for the longest possible period. In effect, that is what most bettors – for whom betting is very definitely an unfavourable game – tend to do.

It is worth noting that, even for a bettor who does not expect to gain from betting, attaining better-than-average performance is, in itself, a worthwhile objective since this spins out available capital longer. The player, overall, is thus able to get more bets for his money, obtaining his pleasure at a lower price.

See Expectation, Favourable game, Probability, Ruin, Utility, Value

Starter's orders

See 'Orders'

Starting prices (SP)

The 'starting prices' or 'SP' are the official odds returned by special press representatives, independent of the bookmaking industry, in attendance at race meetings.

They are based on the betting 'show' shortly before the 'off'. Except where agreed otherwise, starting prices are the basis for settling off-course bets.

SP reporters are not responsible for the shows broadcast in betting shops before a race. These are collected and reported by staff working for SIS, the company responsible for transmitting information and pictures from the racecourse or greyhound track to betting shops.

Stewards' enquiry

Investigation by the Stewards responsible for the conduct of a horse race meeting into any suspected infringement of the rules. The Stewards are empowered, where warranted by circumstances, to alter the placings. Such altered placings become the official result and the normal basis for settling bets. However, some betting shops offer 'first past the post' settlement as an option.

Enquiries are also held into the circumstances of greyhound races where rules may have been infringed but bets are always settled on the actual order of finish – except in the case of void races, in which case stakes are returned without deduction.

See First past the post

Stop-at-a-winner

Instruction to bookmaker to halt a series of bets as soon as a winner is attained. If a non-runner is encountered, the bet continues to the next selection.

Each-way stop-at-a-winner bets continue until one of the selections either occupies or dead-heats for first place.

Straight-up

Wagering on American football matches is mainly handicap betting. So, the winning team, from a betting point of view, is the one that 'covers the spread' – that is to say, is the winner after handicap points have been taken into account. 'Straight-up' refers to the result of a match in terms of points actually scored – *ie* the real result!

See American football, Handicap betting

Strike rate

Number of winning bets to total number of bets – one measure of a bettor's performance (also see 'Return', p. 91). To express as a percentage, calculate thus:

$$\text{strike rate } \% = \frac{\text{number of winners}}{\text{total number of bets}} \times 100$$

Too much attention to strike rate alone tends to deflect from the real issue of gainful betting – the odds returned about the winning bets. For example, a high strike rate of 50% is achievable by backing red-hot stand-out favourites but, if the prices are odds-on, as they are likely to be, then the betting balance sheet is bound to show a

Average odds needed to break-even for different rates of success

(a) % strike rate (*ie* wins per 100 bets)
(b) approx average odds needed to break-even, on-course
(c) approx average odds needed to break-even, allowing for 10% betting shop 'tax'

(a)	(b)	(c)	
50	1/1	6/5	
40	6/4	7/4	approx success rate of jumps favourites
36	7/4	2/1–9/4	approx success rate of flat race favourites
33	2/1	9/4–5/2	approx success rate of 'graded' greyhound favourites
29	5/2	11/4–3/1	approx success rate of newspaper tipsters (horse racing and greyhounds)
25	3/1	7/2	
20	4/1	9/2	
17	5/1	11/2	

loss. On the other hand, a bettor who attains a strike rate of only 20%, but with average odds a shade over 9/2, makes a modest gain, even after 'tax'.

A table of average odds needed to break-even for different strike rates is given on facing page.

Super Heinz

See Multi

Super Yankee

Multiple bet covering 5 selections in different events. Consists of 10 doubles, 10 trebles, 5 fourfolds and 1 fivefold. In all, 26 bets. Also known as a 'Canadian'.

See Multiple bets

Super Yankee (Canadian) staking ready reckoner 5 selections 26 wagers 10 doubles/10 trebles/5 fourfolds/1 fivefold					
Stake	Win	Each-way	Stake	Win	Each-way
0.05	1.30	2.60	0.55	14.30	28.60
0.10	2.60	5.20	0.60	15.60	31.20
0.15	3.90	7.80	0.65	16.90	33.80
0.20	5.20	10.40	0.70	18.20	36.40
0.25	6.50	13.00	0.75	19.50	39.00
0.30	7.80	15.60	0.80	20.80	41.60
0.35	9.10	18.20	0.85	22.10	44.20
0.40	10.40	20.80	0.90	23.40	46.80
0.45	11.70	23.40	0.95	24.70	49.40
0.50	13.00	26.00	1.00	26.00	52.00

Systems

A 'betting system' is a defined set of rules for selecting bets. Even someone who makes selections using a pin is using a system of sorts!

In their favour, systems protect bettors from betting impulsively or on the basis of emotional bias, neither of which contribute to better-than-average performance. In effect, the system operator, having created a set of rules, becomes an automaton putting those rules into effect.

All systems are flawed with the serious defect that they ignore the workings of the human intelligence and its capability of assimilating and integrating *all* the information available about a situation. Anyone who has ever put a system into operation will have experienced the sensation of the inner will tugging against the course of action prescribed by the system rules. To ignore such intimations is a sure way of being led into some wasteful bets. No betting system can hold a candle to the workings of the informed human intelligence. In the end, there is no substitute for a genuine understanding of a betting sport's finer points, familiarity with the abilities of its players, and the capacity to refrain from betting except when the odds look favourable. But that also requires an investment of time and effort, which many people do not want to give – so there will always be those looking for some quick, easy-to-use scheme to fulfil their longings for untold riches from gambling!

Tattersalls Committee

Ruling body on all horse race betting matters with powers to report persons to The Jockey Club who default by not complying with an order of the Committee. Such a person would be liable to be 'warned off' by The Jockey Club and become unable to run horses or attend meetings.

Betting on horse racing is governed by 'Tattersalls Rules', of which Rule 4c, invoked when a runner is withdrawn before coming under orders or declared 'not to have started' but with insufficient time for a new market to be formed, is probably best-known to betting shop customers.

Address: Tattersalls Committee, PO Box 13, 19 Wilwyne Close, Caversham, Reading, Berkshire RG4 0XZ. Telephone: (0734) 461757.

See Disputes, Tattersalls Rule 4c

Tattersalls Rule 4c

Invoked when a horse is withdrawn not under starter's orders or declared 'not to have started' and there is insufficient time to re-form the betting market. It reads (1 January 1992) as follows:

> In the case of bets made at a price on the day of the race before it has been officially notified that a horse has been withdrawn before coming under starter's orders or has been declared 'not to have started', the liability of a layer against any horse remaining in the race, win or place, will be reduced

in accordance with the following scale, depending on the odds current against the withdrawn horse at the time of such official notification.

If the current odds are: (a) 3/10 or longer odds-on by 75p in the £

(b)	2/5 to 1/3	70p in the £
(c)	8/15 to 4/9	65p in the £
(d)	8/13 to 4/7	60p in the £
(e)	4/5 to 4/6	55p in the £
(f)	20/21 to 5/6	50p in the £
(g)	Evens to 6/5	45p in the £
(h)	5/4 to 6/4	40p in the £
(i)	13/8 to 7/4	35p in the £
(j)	15/8 to 9/4	30p in the £
(k)	5/2 to 3/1	25p in the £
(l)	10/3 to 4/1	20p in the £
(m)	9/2 to 11/2	15p in the £
(n)	6/1 to 9/1	10p in the £
(o)	10/1 to 14/1	5p in the £

(p) If over 14/1 the liability would be unchanged

(q) In the case of two or more horses being withdrawn before coming under starter's orders, the total reduction shall not exceed 75p in the £.

Bets made at starting price are not affected, except in cases where insufficient time arises for a fresh market to be formed, when the same scale of reductions will apply.

In the event of the withdrawal of one or more runners in circumstances which would lead to only one runner and therefore a 'walkover', all bets on the race will be void. The race will be considered a 'walkover' for the purpose of settling bets.

For the purpose of this Rule, the non-appearance of the number of a declared runner in the number board will be held to be an official notification of the withdrawal of such horse before coming under starter's orders. In the case of a horse declared by the starter 'not to have started' the race-course announcement will be made to that effect. This official announcement will be made before the race result is displayed.

Tax

Betting shop bets are subject to a 10% deduction called 'tax', of which a large part is government Betting Duty (March 1992 Budget 7¾%, formerly 8%). In the case of horse race bets, part of the difference between Duty and actual rate of deduction is paid to the Horserace Betting Levy Board.

The customer has the option of paying the tax by adding 10% to the stake money when placing the bet, in which case winnings are free of deduction, or of paying tax in the form of a 10% deduction from the returned stake and winnings of successful bets.

Paying tax with the stake is actually marginally advantageous. The bettor who wishes to obtain the benefit of paying tax in this way but who does not wish to invest more than a given basic stake, can do so by *decreasing* the chosen stake by 10%, then adding to that amount the appropriate tax. Here is an example.

For a bet of £10: stake £9 (£10 less 10%)+tax 90p = £9.90. This bet settles exactly the same as a £10 tax unpaid bet, but with a saving of 10p.

No deduction is made from the returns of betting shop computer forecast or tricast bets since an allowance for tax is already included in the declared dividends. For the same reason, no tax should be added to the stake of a computer forecast or tricast bet.

In the case of any-to-come bets, any any-to-come element is technically a separate wager so that, even if tax has been prepaid on the original bet, tax becomes due on winning returns arising from the any-to-come elements.

No Betting Duty is liable on on-course bets, so returns from on-course bookmakers are free of deduction. However, bookmakers at a few greyhound tracks make a controversial deduction of 1% from winning returns, which is passed on to the track promoter as a contribution to the improvement of racing. Racecourse betting shops make a deduction of 6% from returns, 5% of which is passed on to the racecourse (see 'NARBOL', p. 66).

The following table shows, for various basic stakes, how to make the saving of a tax-paid bet without increasing the amount wagered:

Stake	Decreased stake	'Tax'	Saving
£	£	£	£
5.00	4.50	0.45	0.05
10.00	9.00	0.90	0.10
20.00	18.00	1.80	0.20
25.00	22.50	2.25	0.25
50.00	45.00	4.50	0.50
100.00	90.00	9.00	1.00

Through-the-card (T-T-C)

Term indicating that there is a bet on all the races at one meeting. Commonly used in greyhound betting.

The bets go on in racecard order, even if one of the races is declared void and re-run later. If say, the third race is declared void and is re-run at the end of the meeting, it is still deemed, for betting purposes, to be race number 3.

Tipsters

One of the appealing aspects of betting, one would imagine, is the opportunity it provides a keen racing fan to make an autonomous judgement and act upon it. In practice, few bettors wager without a sidelong glance at the opinions of the newspaper tipsters!

Most newspaper tipsters are real experts and their advice comes at an incredibly low price. It is naive to discount, as some writers on betting do, the value of newspaper selections on the grounds that they do not usually show a profit over a whole season.

The tipster can only express his expert opinion as to which runner seems the likeliest winner. *He has no control over the odds at which the runner actually starts.* As stated elsewhere, a bet is only potentially profitable if the odds on offer are greater than the runner's probability of winning (see, 'Value' p. 122). Only a proportion of a tipster's selections could be expected to be 'value' bets and the bettor himself must apply his own intelligence to decide, when he gets a sight of the odds, whether or not a price is favourable. That does not mean that when a given expert's selection starts at surprisingly long odds it is necessarily indicative of value. Experts are human and give the occasional aberrant opinion. Long-shots should always be regarded with caution. However, some tipsters seem to be much more adept than others in terms of the average odds of their winners (see below).

Because bettors *do* take notice of what the press says, this, in itself, tends to bear down on prices – a fact which is especially noticeable when press opinion converges on a single runner.

The overall strike rate of leading newspaper tipsters selecting for every race, is remarkably similar and constant – about 29% – suggesting that this may be an outer limit of forecasting, given the requirements of selecting in every race on the day before. The success rate of 'favourites' is greater – about 36% for flat race favourites – the difference probably being explained by the assimilation by the betting market of unexposed information not at the disposal of the press experts when they make their selections. The effect of such late influences seems to be more pronounced for jumps racing than flat racing and more for flat racing than grey-hounds.

Over a sample period of 6 months, one leading horse race newspaper tipster showed a loss of a mere 3% of theoretical money staked (excluding tax), an astonishing performance given that it included selections for nearly every race, of all degrees of difficulty. His strike rate was 27%. At the other end of the scale, another expert, over the same period, 'lost' 15% for a strike rate of 29%. This illustrates the difference that can exist in average odds between the winners of one expert and another.

Tissue odds

Betting forecast, compiled by a form expert, used by bookmakers as the basis for their 'first show'.

Tote

A pool betting system operated at greyhound tracks and horse race-courses. Greyhound tracks are licensed to operate their own totes (small 't'). At horse racecourses, the tote pools are operated by the Tote (capital 'T') or, in full, the Horserace Totalisator Board, a public body instituted by Act of Parliament in 1928.

In tote betting, all stake money enters a pool and, after permitted deductions for operating expenses and profit, the remainder is shared equitably among holders of winning tickets. Overseas, such betting pools are usually known as 'pari-mutuels'. Strictly speaking, a 'tote' (or 'totalisator') was the machine for counting and register-ing the tickets sold, which today is largely done, much more rapidly and flexibly, by computers.

See Pari-mutuel, Pool betting, Racecourse betting, Tote betting off-course, Tote betting on-course

Tote betting, off-course

A cash betting service at Tote odds off-course is provided by the Tote's betting shop subsidiary, Tote Bookmakers Ltd, and by a number of bookmakers licensed by the Tote to settle bets at Tote odds. New developments on the horizon (see below) are likely to revolutionise Tote betting off-course, but the following describes the situation as it stands at present.

Tote Bookmakers provides access to the on-course Jackpot and Tote Trio, and, except at evening meetings, Placepot pools, and accepts bets at Tote odds Win, Place, and Dual-Forecast.

Bookmakers licensed to bet at Tote odds usually offer Win, Dual-Forecast, Placepot and sometimes Place.

Since these Tote Win, Place, Dual-Forecast, and Placepot bets off-course do not necessarily participate in the on-course pools, they are settled, in the absence of a dividend (or in the dual-forecast where the dividend is paid on 'the 1st or 2nd with any other horse'), on an SP or computer forecast basis.

Except for Tote Bookmakers, off-course bets at Tote odds may be subject to special limits. Win, Place and Dual-Forecast payouts are sometimes limited to a given multiple of the SP or CSF. This protects the bookmaker from the occasional freak dividend, although it has to be said that the possibility of an unexpected bumper payout is one of the attractions of betting with the Tote!

Returns from off-course bets at Tote dividends are subject to the normal betting shop 'tax' deduction.

The Tote has developed a sophisticated terminal system, shortly to be introduced into Tote Bookmakers' and some other bookmakers' betting shops. These will provide direct access to racecourse pools providing bettors with a new basis for pool betting off-course, and opening the way for the introduction of a huge-payout weekend 'superbet'.

Tote betting, on-course

The Tote operates Win, Place, Dual-Forecast and Placepot pools at all horse race meetings. The Jackpot and Trio pools are operated at major meetings.

The minimum unit stake on the Win, Place and Dual-Forecast pools is £2, but £1 each-way is accepted in some enclosures. £1 Dual-Forecast combination bets are accepted in all enclosures.

Jackpot and Placepot minimum stake per single line is £1 but permutations of 10p per line and upwards are accepted for total stakes of not less than £1.

The Win pool operates on all races, Dual-Forecast on all races with 3 or more runners, and the Place pool on all races with 5 or more runners. Place dividends are paid as follows:

> Handicaps 16 or more runners 1–2–3–4
> All races 8 or more runners   1–2–3
> All races 5, 6, or 7 runners   1–2

A Dual-Forecast is a winner if the 2 selections finish 1st and 2nd in either order. If there is no correct forecast, the dividend is declared on the winner and second with any other.

In the Win, Place and Dual-Forecast pools, stakes are refunded if the selection is withdrawn without coming under starter's orders or is declared 'not to have started'.

Jackpot and Placepot pools operate on 6 nominated races. If not won outright, the pool is carried forward. If there is a part winner, the balance of the pool is carried forward.

In the Jackpot and Placepot, a stake on a non-runner is put on the

SP favourite. If there is more than one favourite, the bet goes on the favourite with the lowest racecard number.

In the Tote Trio, the bettor is asked to nominate the first 3 finishers *in any order.* The Trio operates on selected races and the minimum stake is £1.

Bettors unable to cash a ticket on the day of racing or on the following day of the same fixture can claim by sending it to: Horserace Totalisator Board, Racecourse Division, 45 Hanworth Road, Sunbury-on-Thames, Middlesex TW16 5DA.

The dividends declared by the Tote include a £1 stake.

The deductions from each pool are as follows: Win 16%, Place 24%, Dual-Forecast 29%, Trio 26%, Jackpot 26%, and Placepot 26%.

Tote Dual-Forecast

The bettor selects the runners to finish 1st and 2nd, in either order. The pool operates in all races of 3 or more runners. Retention 29%. If there are no winning bets in the pool for the 1st and 2nd combined, the dividend is paid on the winning horse with any other and the second horse with any other. Minimum stake: £2. £1 combination accepted.

See Tote betting off-course, Tote betting on-course

Tote Jackpot

Pool operated by the Tote at major fixtures in which the bettor is asked to nominate the winners of 6 selected races, usually the first 6 races. Unwon pools are carried forward. There is a minimum single-line stake of £1 but permutations of 10p and upwards are accepted for total stakes of not less than £1. Tote Jackpot bets, with access to the racecourse pool, may be made off-course with the Tote's betting shop subsidiary Tote Bookmakers.

See Tote betting off-course, Tote betting on-course

Tote Place

The bettor selects a runner to be placed, as follows: handicaps 16 or more runners 1-2-3-4, 8 or more runners 1-2-3, 5-7 runners 1-2. Fewer than 5 runners, the Place pool does not operate, unless the field is reduced by a late withdrawal, in which case the dividend is paid on the winning horse. Retention 24%. The net pool is equally divided by the number of qualifying places, then further divided by the respective number of units for each placed horse. Thus, there is a different dividend for each of the placed runners. If the calculated dividend falls below 0.70p, the minimum place dividend is £1.00. Minimum stake: £2 (however, £1 each-way is accepted in some enclosures).

See Tote betting off-course, Tote betting on-course

Table of Tote dividends and their odds-equivalent from 1/10 to 100/1. All Tote dividends are inclusive of a £1 unit stake

Tote Dividend £	Nearest SP	Tote Dividend £	Nearest SP	Tote Dividend £	Nearest SP
1 10	1/10	3 30	9/4	7 50	13/2
1 20	1/5	3 40	5/2	8 00	7/1
1 30	3/10	3 50	5/2	8 50	15/2
1 40	2/5	3 60	5/2	9 00	8/1
1 50	1/2	3 70	11/4	9 50	17/2
1 60	8/13	3 80	11/4	10 00	9/1
1 70	8/11	3 90	3/1	11 00	10/1
1 80	4/5	4 00	3/1	12 00	11/1
1 90	10/11	4 10	3/1	13 00	12/1
2 00	Evens	4 20	10/3	14 00	13/1
2 10	11/10	4 30	10/3	15 00	14/1
2 20	6/5	4 40	10/3	17 00	16/1
2 30	5/4	4 50	7/2	19 00	18/1
2 40	11/8	4 60	7/2	21 00	20/1
2 50	6/4	4 70	7/2	23 00	22/1
2 60	13/8	4 80	4/1	26 00	25/1
2 70	7/4	4 90	4/1	29 00	28/1
2 80	7/4	5 00	4/1	34 00	33/1
2 90	15/8	5 50	9/2	41 00	40/1
3 00	2/1	6 00	5/1	51 00	50/1
3 10	85/40	6 50	11/2	67 00	66/1
3 20	9/4	7 00	6/1	101 00	100/1

Tote Placepot

Pool operated by the Tote at all meetings, in which the bettor is asked to nominate a placed horse in each of 6 selected races, usually races 1–6. Unwon pools go forward.

There is a minimum single-line stake of £1 but permutations of 10p and upwards are accepted for total stakes of not less than £1.

Tote Placepot bets may be made off-course with the Tote's betting shop subsidiary Tote Bookmakers and with certain bookmakers who are licensed by the Tote to take bets at Tote odds. Where a Placepot dividend is not declared at the racecourse, Placepot bets are settled as place accumulators on an SP basis. The

bookmaker's rules should be checked.
See Tote betting off-course, Tote betting on-course

Tote Trio

A new pool, introduced in 1991, at first at selected meetings.

The bettor is asked to nominate the runners to finish 1st, 2nd and 3rd in any order. If there is no correct combination, the bet is settled on the basis of anyone nominating 2 out of the first 3 finishers. A minimum field of 8 runners is required to operate. The retention is 26%.

The minimum stake on- and off-course is £1. No stakes in combinations of less than £1 are accepted.

The bet is available to the Tote's credit customers and at Tote Bookmakers' betting shops off-course.
See Tote betting off-course, Tote betting on-course

Tote Win

The bettor selects the runner to finish 1st. Retention 16%. Guaranteed minimum dividend of £1.10. If winner unbacked, stakes refunded in full. Minimum stake: £2.
See Tote betting off-course, Tote betting on-course

Tout

A person who spies on racehorses in training and/or attempts to cull information from employees of training establishments for the purpose either of selling the information or for placing bets. As racing has become more open, so the role of touts has diminished.

Literally, 'to tout' means 'to spy on', a slang word going back to at least 1700.

Trainer's selected

Term used to select a trainer's preferred runner where 2 or more from the same stable are running in the same race – deemed to be whichever starts at the shortest price. If 2 or more share the same lowest price, the stake is divided between them.

Trap number

In greyhound racing, the runners start from numbered boxes indicated in advance on the racecard.

Selections may be made by stating trap number alone, without the name of the selection. This is convenient for those bettors whose betting strategy is based on following certain trap numbers or groups of trap numbers. But, unless the bettor wishes to be on a particular trap, come what may, selections should be given by name. Selections made by trap number alone are on that trap even if the greyhound scheduled to run is replaced by a reserve – a not infrequent occurrence.

Betting by trap number is very popular – especially in such bets as 'through-the-card' forecast doubles and trebles. The method may deliver, by chance, some spectacular wins – but, as a form of betting, it replaces skill with the whims of fate!

Trap numbers, in themselves, are not form. Statistics show that any advantage enjoyed by certain trap positions at a track is usually only slight and, from the greyhound's point of view, quite out-weighed by the advantage of being the best runner in the field.

See Greyhound betting

Treble

Bet in which 3 selections, in different events, are linked so that the total return (stake+winnings) from each successive leg is auto-matically restaked on the next leg. All 3 selections must succeed for the bet to pay a return.

See Accumulator

Tricast

A tricast is similar to a forecast but requires the bettor to nominate the 3 runners to finish 1st, 2nd and 3rd in correct order. It is available on certain horse races (handicaps of 8 or more declared runners and no fewer than 4 actual runners) and on BAGS grey-hound races of 6 or more runners, when an official computer tricast return is made.

Only singles – not doubles or trebles – are allowed.

Most betting shop clients making this bet like to improve their chance by increasing their cover with permutations.

Special printed tricast slips make this bet easier to write, especially where permutations are involved.

The computer tricast dividend is inclusive of an allowance for tax, so no tax should be added to the stake. Nor is there any deduction from the return.

If one of the tricast selections is a non-runner, the bet is settled as a straight forecast on the remaining 2 selections on the slip. If there are 2 non-runners, the bet is settled as a win single at SP, tax being payable on the return.

If a tricast bet is taken in error on a race in which no tricast is operated, the bet is settled as a straight forecast on the first two runners named on the slip.

The equivalent bet to a tricast on a greyhound totalisator is usually known as a 'trio'.

To cover several selections in one race all-ways requires the following numbers of bets:

3 selections	6 tricasts/trios
4 selections	24 tricasts/trios
5 selections	60 tricasts/trios
6 selections	120 tricasts/trios

Triesta

A dual-forecast (1st and 2nd in either order) treble, requiring only one stake, on specified greyhound races. The winning return, which includes an allowance for tax, is announced after the 3rd leg. There are also consolation dividends.

The return and specified races depend upon the firm marketing the bet. The special rules to govern various contingencies are usually printed on the reverse of the special printed slips which are supplied.

Most bettors like to improve their chance in this difficult bet with permutations.

One 'major' offers dual-forecast trebles on any 3 greyhound races not precluded by its rules. For settling purposes, the BAGS computer forecast dividend or Chart dividend is halved.

Permutation guide: The number of dual-forecasts per race for different numbers of selections is as follows.

2 selections	1 dual-forecast
3 selections	3 dual-forecasts
4 selections	6 dual-forecasts
5 selections	10 dual-forecasts
6 selections	15 dual-forecasts

To find how many bets in a Triesta (or other dual-forecast treble), multiply together the number of dual-forecast bets required for each race. For example, if there are 2 selections in the first race (1 dual-forecast), 3 selections in the second race (3 dual-forecasts) and 4 selections in the third race (6 dual-forecasts), there are $1 \times 3 \times 6$ bets = 18 bets in all.

Trio

Name of the tote pool at a greyhound track in which the bettor is required to select the runners to finish 1st, 2nd and 3rd in correct order. The equivalent of the betting shop bet known as a 'tricast'. For permutation guide, see 'Tricast' starting on p. 117.
See Tote Trio

Trixie

Simple and popular full-cover multiple bet consisting of 4 wagers from 3 selections (A,B,C). Thus, 3 doubles (AB, AC, BC) and 1 treble (ABC).

See Multiple bets

Trixie staking ready reckoner 3 selections 4 wagers 3 doubles/1 treble					
Stake	**Win**	**Each-way**	**Stake**	**Win**	**Each-way**
0.05	0.20	0.40	0.55	2.20	4.40
0.10	0.40	0.80	0.60	2.40	4.80
0.15	0.60	1.20	0.65	2.60	5.20
0.20	0.80	1.60	0.70	2.80	5.60
0.25	1.00	2.00	0.75	3.00	6.00
0.30	1.20	2.40	0.80	3.20	6.40
0.35	1.40	2.80	0.85	3.40	6.80
0.40	1.60	3.20	0.90	3.60	7.20
0.45	1.80	3.60	0.95	3.80	7.60
0.50	2.00	4.00	1.00	4.00	8.00

Twist

See Patent

Underdog

American football betting jargon for the lesser-fancied of two teams set to play each other, the preferred team being the 'favourite'. In press reports, sometimes merely 'dog'.

See American football

Under-round

The opposite of 'over-round'. Describes a set of odds biassed in favour of the bettor at the expense of the bookmaker.

See Odds, Over-broke, Over-round

Understaking

Understaking occurs when the total paid and receipted on a betting slip is insufficient to cover all the bets written.

Such errors are normally resolved by settling the whole of the slip in proportion.

See Overstaking

Under starter's orders

See 'Orders'

Unfavourable game

Mathematical term for a betting proposition in which the player has a negative expectation of gain. In commercially promoted games, such as those played in casinos or racing and sports betting, the games are, overall, unfavourable to the bettor.

See Expectation, Fair bet, Favourable game

Union Jack

Limited cover multiple bet consisting of 8 trebles from 9 selections. (A, B, C, D, E, F, G, H, I). The trebles can be visualised in Union Jack format (hence the name): ABC, DEF, GHI, ADG, BEH, CFI, AEI, CEG (see diagram).

The Union Jack covers only 8 of the 84 possible trebles in 9 selections so there is plenty of scope for disappointment in this bet. How the bet fares depends much on the success of selection E since this features in 4 of the trebles.

Notwithstanding its limitations, this bet has proved popular because it offers the excitement of the possibility of a large win for a modest outlay.

A Union Jack can be win or each-way.

See Limited cover

Union Jack staking ready reckoner 9 selections 8 wagers 8 trebles (limited cover)					
Stake	Win	Each-way	Stake	Win	Each-way
0.05	0.40	0.80	0.55	4.40	8.80
0.10	0.80	1.60	0.60	4.80	9.60
0.15	1.20	2.40	0.65	5.20	10.40
0.20	1.60	3.20	0.70	5.60	11.20
0.25	2.00	4.00	0.75	6.00	12.00
0.30	2.40	4.80	0.80	6.40	12.80
0.35	2.80	5.60	0.85	6.80	13.60
0.40	3.20	6.40	0.90	7.20	14.40
0.45	3.60	7.20	0.95	7.60	15.20
0.50	4.00	8.00	1.00	8.00	16.00

Unnamed selections

Unnamed selections are those using such devices as 'favourite', 'trainer's selected', 'owner's selected', and 'jockey's mount', in which the bettor is attaching importance to information not necessarily known at the time of placing the bet.

The use of the term 'favourite' without clear instructions can lead to all kinds of misunderstanding. Betting shop rules usually contain provisions for investing stakes where instructions are incomplete or ambiguous – not necessarily what the bettor intended! To avoid disappointment, take care to state time and meeting.

In greyhound racing, betting by trap number is very common. Where this is the case, the bettor is on the greyhound running from that trap even if a reserve dog is running in the place of the greyhound on the racecard. If both name and trap number are given, name takes precedence, so that, if the dog is withdrawn, the bettor is on a non-runner and the stake is returned.

See Favourite, Incorrect instructions

Up-and-down

A 'stakes-about' bet.

See Double-stakes-about, Single-stakes-about

Utility

Rational beings do not take risks for nothing. 'Utility' is a term used in mathematics to represent the usefulness of a given risk to the risk-taker.

In the mathematical theory of gambling, it is assumed that a person making a decision under risk conditions (*ie* betting on an outcome) acts in a manner to maximise the value of the utility. If utility were an *objective* quality, there would be a straightforward relationship between (1) the degree to which the prize would add to present wealth, (2) the degree to which the stake, if lost, would deplete present wealth, and (3) the likelihood of success or failure.

Objective criteria do enter, *to an extent*, into bettors' calculations of utility – but it is not the whole story. Since bookmakers receive more money in lost stakes than they pay out in winnings, the betting public, taken as a whole, is a net loser. So where is the utility?

The gap is filled by what is termed 'subjective utility': excitement, entertainment, feelings of participation, in the case of bets offering big payouts for small stakes the hope of deliverance from the daily round, and so on – depending on the individual.

Those responsible for making strategic decisions regarding the regulation of betting should recognise that utility is not a value whose price is without limit. Increases in taxes or deductions which push the price of betting beyond the value of the utility to the consumer lead inevitably to lost turnover.

Value

Although we may bet, first and foremost, for fun and entertainment, part of the enjoyment is trying to make a gain. Finding 'winners', in itself, will not necessarily lead to that desirable end. A good strike rate of 1 winner in 3, for example, will still lead to long-term loss if the average odds of those winners is less than 2/1 (or less than 5/2 in the case of betting shop bets on which tax has to be paid).

To improve our chance of making a gain, we must concentrate our attention, not merely on finding winners, but on finding winners whose odds contain an element of 'value'.

'Value' is a term much used in betting but its real meaning is commonly misunderstood. It does not, for example, mean a runner at long odds. 6/4, 1/1 or even odds-on may be good value. It depends on circumstances. In fact, outsiders in horse and greyhound racing are generally very bad value. Statistics show that on long-priced runners the average margin of profit for bookmakers is much greater than on those at short prices. Little value, therefore, is to be expected among the outside chances in those sports. The same does not necessarily hold in other sports betting.

To understand value, one must first distinguish between the 'price', meaning the terms of the payout if a bet is successful, and the 'chance', meaning the likelihood of the bet succeeding. The potential for confusion is ever present because the term 'odds' and the same notation (*ie* 1/1, 6/4, 2/1, and so on) are used for both entities.

Value is the difference between a contender's *chance* and the *price*. If the price offered is less than the actual chance (say 1/1 for a 2/1 chance) then there is 'bad value'. But if the price is greater than the chance (say, 5/2 for a 1/1 chance), then there is 'good value'. Whatever selection method is used, the bettor can only hope to make a gain by following the principle of looking for value.

Allowing that the betting industry is geared to make a profit from its customers, not the reverse, it is only to be expected that prices, by their nature, are usually in the bad value category!

However, betting on sports is not the same as betting on gambling artefacts such as dice or roulette wheels, where the true odds for any bet can be known exactly. The odds for the contenders in a sporting event are opinions – the opinions of the bookmakers' odds compilers and the opinions of the public whose betting preferences cause prices to fluctuate. Opinions, of their nature, can be wayward, and odds which underestimate the merit of a contender do appear, surprisingly often.

There are many reasons why prices may, on occasions, part company with the evidence of the form book. Disproportionately large bets by enthusiasts (such as an over-optimistic owner backing his own runner), rumour, sentiment, patriotic fervour, media hype, even appealing names – these are a few of the influences that can randomly influence the shape of the betting market.

It is not necessary for the value-hunting bettor always to understand the reason for an inappropriate price although any such insight may inspire greater confidence. It is merely necessary to stick by the evidence of form – the only reasonable basis for estimating winning chances – and convert what it tells into one's own estimate of the true odds, to use as a yardstick for comparison with the price on offer. The technique is not precise, but it is surprising how startlingly apparent anomalous prices can be, once one is on the look-out for them.

All this presupposes sufficient knowledge of the sport in question to make sound judgements. Value is created by the unwisdom of others, so it follows that, if one is to graduate as a successful value-hunting bettor, one must be correspondingly wise – by acquiring insight into the finer points of the sport and thorough familiarity with its players, whether horses, greyhounds or people.

Another essential quality of the value-hunter is the capacity to let races or events go by without betting. Value should not be expected from every event. One should certainly expect to experience more non-betting than betting occasions.

The bettor, in his search for value, should not fall into the trap of believing that it is possible to quantify chances with precision. A discussion of the issues is given in the article on 'Probability', starting on p. 82. Suffice it to say here that the bettor should concentrate on palpable value, odds which from an informed viewpoint seem to *stand out* as value bets. There is no way of knowing, for any given occasion, whether one has been right or wrong in one's judgement. What the value-seeking bettor sets out to do is, by virtue of exercising intelligent appraisal, bet only when the odds *appear* to offer a margin of value, in the anticipation of a margin of value *over the long term* as reflected by a little gain. The bettor can never know which bets contributed how much to the long-term result.

Since the bettor must depend very largely upon the integrative reasoning powers of his brain, it may be found useful to construct a scale for converting into numbers the degrees of *verbal* conviction which are the currency the brain uses. This can provide a useful means of calibrating opinions and of testing their credibility (see below). However, the act of turning verbal statements of conviction into percentage or odds form should not imply any gain in precision. An opinion remains an opinion, prone to the same errors, whether handled in number or verbal form. Here is a suggested scheme.

	Chance	Odds
No chance	0	*
Poor chance	10%	10/1
Moderate chance	20%	4/1
Good chance	30%	2/1
Very good chance	40%	6/4
Even chance	50%	1/1
Odds-on chance	60%	4/6

The figures in the centre column are approximate 'percentage chances' (see table on p. 70) – a means of expressing chance in the form of numbers on a scale of 0 to 100. 0 equals 'no chance at all' and 100 equals 'certainty'. All the other chances lie between. The sign '%' is a reminder that a scale of 100 is being used.

The usefulness of percentages is that they provide a means of checking the overall credibility of a set of odds. Since 100 equals certainty, a set of estimated chances, when added up, must total 100. In this context, figures such as 110 or 90 make no sense at all.

As a simple example, let us look at a coin-spinning situation:

Heads	Even chance	50%
Tails	Even chance	50%
Total	**Certainty**	**100%**

The table on p. 124 indicates only 'round number' chances. Extra flexibility can be supplied by the following in-between odds: 35% (7/4), 25% (3/1), 15% (5/1) and 5% (20/1). But, again, one must necessarily be careful not to introduce spurious finesse to a process which, after all, is based on approximations.

To facilitate understanding, the percentage/odds equivalents given in the scheme are approximate.

If the percentages are applied to bookmakers' payout odds (*ie* prices), it will be found that the total exceeds 100. This simply reflects the fact that bookmakers' odds are not probabilities but terms on which they are offering to settle bets.

See Odds

Void bet

Invalid bet. The stake is returnable in full, without deduction.

Walkover

A race in which there is only one runner. For settlement purposes, any selection involved is treated as a non-runner.

Weigh-in

The weighed-in signal is the point at which the right of settlement to a horse race bet becomes official.

Winning streaks

See Losing streaks

Withdrawal

See Late withdrawal, Tattersalls Rule 4c

'Without' bookmaker

A racecourse bookmaker (either horses or greyhounds) who specialises in making a book *without* the probable favourite. The name of the horse or greyhound to be omitted is deleted from the list of runners and a book is made around the remaining runners.

The 'without' bookmaker pays out (1) if the bettor's selection wins the race or (2) if the bettor's selection is second to the omitted runner. If the bettor's selection dead-heats for first place with the omitted runner, the bookmaker pays out in full. If it dead-heats in a winning position with any other runner, the normal dead-heat rule applies – the payout is to one-half the stake.

With the field

An instruction indicating that a selection should be coupled with all the other contenders in the event. For example, 'Trap 3 with the field' is a request for the following 5 forecast combinations (in a 6-dog race): 3-1, 3-2, 3-4, 3-5, and 3-6. The bet may be reversed. 'Trap 3 to be second to the field' indicates bets as follows: 1-3, 2-3, 4-3, 5-3 and 6-3.

Yankee

Multiple bet covering 4 selections in different events. Consists of 6 doubles, 4 trebles and 1 fourfold. In all, 11 bets.
See Multiple bets

Yankee staking ready reckoner 4 selections 11 wagers 6 doubles/4 trebles/1 fourfold					
Stake	Win	Each-way	Stake	Win	Each-way
0.05	0.55	1.10	0.55	6.05	12.10
0.10	1.10	2.20	0.60	6.60	13.20
0.15	1.65	3.30	0.65	7.15	14.30
0.20	2.20	4.40	0.70	7.70	15.40
0.25	2.75	5.50	0.75	8.25	16.50
0.30	3.30	6.60	0.80	8.80	17.60
0.35	3.85	7.70	0.85	9.35	18.70
0.40	4.40	8.80	0.90	9.90	19.80
0.45	4.95	9.90	0.95	10.45	20.90
0.50	5.50	11.00	1.00	11.00	22.00

Returns Ready Reckoner

(inclusive of stake)

£1 Stake SP	Win	Place 1/5	Place 1/4	Dead-heat or jt-fav (of two)
1/5	1 20	1 04	1 05	60
2/9	1 22	1 04	1 06	61
1/4	1 25	1 05	1 06	63
2/7	1 29	1 06	1 07	64
30/100	1 30	1 06	1 08	65
1/3	1 33	1 07	1 08	67
4/11	1 36	1 07	1 09	68
2/5	1 40	1 08	1 10	70
4/9	1 44	1 09	1 11	72
40/85	1 47	1 09	1 12	74
1/2	1 50	1 10	1 13	75
8/15	1 53	1 11	1 13	77
4/7	1 57	1 11	1 14	79
8/13	1 62	1 12	1 15	81
4/6	1 67	1 13	1 17	83
8/11	1 73	1 15	1 18	86
4/5	1 80	1 16	1 20	90
5/6	1 83	1 17	1 21	92
10/11	1 91	1 18	1 23	95
20/21	1 95	1 19	1 24	98
evens	2 00	1 20	1 25	1 00
21/20	2 05	1 21	1 26	1 03
11/10	2 10	1 22	1 28	1 05
6/5	2 20	1 24	1 30	1 10
5/4	2 25	1 25	1 31	1 13
11/8	2 38	1 28	1 34	1 19
6/4	2 50	1 30	1 38	1 25
13/8	2 63	1 33	1 41	1 31
7/4	2 75	1 35	1 44	1 38
15/8	2 88	1 38	1 47	1 44
2/1	3 00	1 40	1 50	1 50
85/40	3 13	1 43	1 53	1 56
9/4	3 25	1 45	1 56	1 63
5/2	3 50	1 50	1 63	1 75
11/4	3 75	1 55	1 69	1 88
3/1	4 00	1 60	1 75	2 00
100/30	4 33	1 67	1 83	2 17
7/2	4 50	1 70	1 88	2 25
4/1	5 00	1 80	2 00	2 50
9/2	5 50	1 90	2 13	2 75
5/1	6 00	2 00	2 25	3 00
11/2	6 50	2 10	2 38	3 25
6/1	7 00	2 20	2 50	3 50
13/2	7 50	2 30	2 63	3 75
7/1	8 00	2 40	2 75	4 00
15/2	8 50	2 50	2 88	4 25
8/1	9 00	2 60	3 00	4 50
17/2	9 50	2 70	3 13	4 75
9/1	10 00	2 80	3 25	5 00
10/1	11 00	3 00	3 50	5 50
11/1	12 00	3 20	3 75	6 00
12/1	13 00	3 40	4 00	6 50
14/1	15 00	3 80	4 50	7 50
16/1	17 00	4 20	5 00	8 50
18/1	19 00	4 60	5 50	9 50
20/1	21 00	5 00	6 00	10 50
25/1	26 00	6 00	7 25	13 00
33/1	34 00	7 60	9 25	17 00
40/1	41 00	9 00	11 00	20 50
50/1	51 00	11 00	13 50	25 50

To deduct tax at 10%, multiply by 0.90